Stitched Pho

Mosaic Quilting

Stitched Photo Mosaic Quilting

Landauer Publishing, www.landauerpub.com,
is an imprint of Fox Chapel Publishing Company, Inc.

Project Team
Managing Editor: Gretchen Bacon
Acquisition Editor: Amelia Johanson
Editor: Sherry Vitolo
Copy Editor: Joseph Borden
Designer: Llara Pazdan
Indexer: Jean Bissell

ISBN 978-1-947163-95-9

Library of Congress Control Number: 2022937807

We are always looking for talented authors.
To submit an idea, please send a brief inquiry to
acquisitions@foxchapelpublishing.com.

Printed in China
Second printing

Dedication

This book is dedicated to my crafty family and to my not-so-crafty, but
always supportive husband.

Special thanks to Sadie, who took photos, made drawings, and read
early versions of this book more times than she cared to.

Stitched Photo
Mosaic Quilting

A Unique Grid Technique for Piecing Images into Beautiful Quilts

TIMNA TARR

Landauer Publishing

Contents

Introduction

Stitched mosaic quilting is an art form and like all such crafts, my process developed through a combination of inspiration, influence, and creation.

Inspiration

This inspiring photo of my cousin's daughter perfectly captures her spunky toddler attitude.

The photo above is what started me on my stitched mosaic journey. My cousin captured his daughter as a quintessential two-year-old. Her round toddler belly, the electrical tape on the bridge of her glasses, and her full-face squint to keep the sun out of her eyes all made me laugh out loud. As soon as I saw this photo, I was inspired to make a quilt based on it.

Wanting to make a portrait quilt and knowing how to do it are two very different things. The idea of creating an image of a person, especially a face, was terrifying. I was completely intimidated and did not know how to begin. Up until that point, the only representational quilts I had made were of maps, which are basically abstract works. No one really cares if the landmarks on a quilted map are accurate or not, but someone may care if their eyes are off-kilter. Over my quilting life, I have read about different techniques for making portrait quilts, but those methods did not work for me. I knew I needed to come up with a process that was engaging for my brain but did not require deft drafting skills.

Influence

It's funny how the art gods have their way of pointing us in the right direction. The same summer I saw the inspiring photo of my cousin's daughter I had also been spending a lot of time looking at Chuck Close's paintings. I have long admired Close's work, ever since I saw one of his portraits in a 1999 show at the University of Massachusetts Museum of Contemporary Art. While I had learned about Close's work in my art history classes in college and had seen them in museums, it wasn't until 1999 when I saw his piece in this show, hung alongside other contemporary artists' work, that I really grasped what Close was doing with his oversized portraits. He painted giant faces that stared down at the viewer, prompting the viewer to stare back. Ordinary faces become monumental and powerful under his care.

Close also kept his reference grids visible in his finished work, integrating the grid into the composition. Artists throughout time have used grids to help copy and resize images, but often the grid is erased or painted over so the viewer never sees the underpinnings of the artwork. Keeping the grid in a piece of art is no different from arranging quilt blocks into a grid. The grid is both part of the underlying structure and part of the visual aesthetic. I started my quilting life as a traditional block-based quilter, so it only seemed natural for me to think about retaining a grid while making a portrait quilt.

Creation

When I made map quilts, I enlarged the printed map to the finished size of the quilt and used the large print as the pattern. With that precedent, and knowing that I wanted the portrait quilt to be larger than life, I had the photo of my young cousin printed larger than life-sized and decided to use that photo as a pattern.

Without much of a plan, I drew a 2" (5.1cm) diagonal grid right on top of the enlarged photo. I knew if I could figure out how to make one 2" square, I could make a second 2" square, and then a third. Once I had a row of blocks, I could sew them together just like in any other quilt. In this case, the grid is not only used to change the size of the finished piece but also to break the image up into small components, much like a tile mosaic. I do not like to plan out a whole big project at once, but I am good at accomplishing small, manageable steps that get me to my goal. With all of that in mind, I started making freezer paper templates and machine appliquéing pieces together. I started with the minor details: the fish, the T-shirt, and the shadow. By the time I got to my young cousin's face, my technique was figured out. That doesn't mean working on her face wasn't terrifying. It was. But I trusted the process, and, in the end, I was happy with the result.

The result of a successful blending of inspiration and process: *Up Close and Personal.*

When *Up Close and Personal* was completed, my cousin showed a photo of the quilt to his daughter. Her response was, "It looks like me!" I knew I was on to something. If she could recognize herself in the quilt, I'd accomplished my goal. I became obsessed with the idea of making more portraits and immediately went over to a friend's house to take photos of her chickens for my next stitched mosaic project. *Clucking Awesome: Bonnie and Princess* on page 11 is the result of that photoshoot. After the chickens came a pig, then a cow, and then those quilts became part of a twelve-part series of barnyard animals called *Noble Menagerie* (see page 8).

Stitched mosaic quilting is a prepared-edge appliqué technique, meaning that the appliqué edges are turned under and, except for a few tiny details, there are no unsewn raw fabric edges visible in the finished quilt. This process is satisfying and achievable even for those new to portraits because you do not need to know how to draw to make a photo-realistic quilt, and each step is broken down into tiny, bite-sized pieces. With a few basic sewing skills, a photo to work from, some fabric,

Gallery

Noble Menagerie Series

The Noble Menagerie Series is a series of 12 barnyard animal portraits I created that were featured as a cohesive exhibit at both the International Quilt Festival and the Texas Quilt Museum. The series was also the basis of my first fabric line of the same name, printed by Studio e. The original photos used for this series were enlarged and printed at 40" x 40" (1 x 1m).

The Royal Ruminant

How does one contain a Nubian goat, literally and figuratively? Add a fence. The diagonal line that the fence created enhanced the composition. Without the diagonal of the fence, the quilt looked flat. I made the fence blue to complement the orange background.

Finished quilt size 38" x 38" (96.5 x 96.5cm)

One challenge with this quilt was that when I added the catchlight to his eyes, he did not come alive like the others. His expression was flat. Then I examined my original photo more closely and realized that the catchlights in his eyes were squares rather than circles. As soon as I changed the shape of the catchlights, he livened right up. Goats have rectangular pupils, a fact I did not know at the time. When

Taking a second look at my original reference photo allowed me to find the secret of capturing goat eyes: they have rectangular catchlights!

The Cowntess of Cud

This quilt is highly edited from the original photo. I removed the stanchion and the brown cow but left the main subject's tongue sticking out. Included are fabrics that made me laugh. One piece on her forehead says, "moo moo moo," there is a bra on the top of her head, and there are several farm- and cow-related prints sprinkled throughout. Do not be afraid to use your novelty fabrics!

Finished quilt size 36" x 36" (91.4 x 91.4cm)

The Queen of Calico

Caleigh was an endlessly inquisitive cat. Living with her was always entertaining and sometimes annoying. I took this photo while she was sitting on my lap, which is appropriate since she loved to be in the middle of everyone's business. Picking out the slightly pink fabrics above her nose and the green fabrics for her eyes was really fun. The eyes, while intimidating, were not hard to make since they are composed of larger pieces of fabric. I find the smaller an eye is, the harder it is to replicate.

Finished quilt size 37" x 37" (94 x 94cm)

Mother Clucker

How great is that green crate? This rooster was at the local Three County Fair, and he is as handsome as they come. Notice that, even though he is a black rooster, I did not stick to only black fabrics in his feathers. There are some blue, purple, and brown fabrics. As long as a fabric is dark, it can "read" as black. Don't tell the other animals, but he is my favorite.

Finished quilt size 36" x 36" (91.4 x 91.4cm)

Lady Teela, of Amherst

I took many pictures of my sister's dog, Teela, who looked at me indifferently in every single one. Teela showed her big grin when my sister was behind the camera, though. The lesson with this quilt: enlist help when needed. And, to be perfectly honest, dog teeth are pesky to make. You will notice that the *Dashing Dog* on page 95 and *Daisy the Corgi* on page 16 have only a few key teeth in the final quilts because I find teeth to be troublesome.

Finished quilt size 38" x 38" (96.5 x 96.5cm)

King of the Corral

Caine is a working draft horse who now lives in Kansas. I was told that his teammate and uncle, Pete, is the brains of the duo, while Caine likes to look pretty. He does a good job of that! The challenge with this white horse is that he does not have much value or color change in his coat. I tried to play up the blonde in his mane and the gray on his nose. While Caine's chest isn't actually green, the dark value created the shadow I was looking for. In the background, I experimented with making a more regimented color layout than I usually do, using only solid fabrics.

Finished quilt size 37" x 37" (94 x 94cm)

Clucking Awesome: Bonnie and Princess

Bonnie and Princess are the local chickens that started me on this journey of stitching barnyard animals. Every quilt teaches us something, and this quilt showed me that I did not need to be completely faithful to the original photograph. If I were to make this quilt again, I would focus only on Bonnie, who is looking straight at the camera. Removing Princess, the fence, and the horizon line would create a stronger composition. In later quilts in this series, you will see how I learned to edit out extraneous details.

Finished quilt size 36" x 36" (91.4 x 91.4cm)

The Marquess of Muscovy

"Floral fabrics" was the rule I followed for the background of this quilt. I cut 2½" (6.4cm) squares of all the floral fabrics in my stash. When I ran out of flowers, I cut into fabrics that were flower-like. The florals have a similar visual texture to the gravel the duck is standing on in the original photo, which was a happy accident.

The most challenging part about making color decisions for this quilt was creating enough value contrast between the background and the duck's bill. The bill kept getting lost in the flowers, so I intensified the orange to encourage the bill to stand out.

Finished quilt size 38" x 38" (96.5 x 96.5cm)

Here is what the background looked like when I was auditioning fabric placement before anything was sewn together.

The Llord of Llamas

Purple was the obvious choice for the background color of this regal animal. I love that when I quilted in his white flyaway hairs, they showed up beautifully against the darker background.

Finished quilt size 38" x 38" (96.5 x 96.5cm)

The fur details I often add with quilting are very noticeable on the dark background of this particular quilt.

The Hare Apparent

Overall, this is not a great photo, but the expression on the rabbit's face charmed me. By ignoring the bars of the cage, the dignity and curiosity of the rabbit come through in the final quilt.

Finished quilt size 38" x 38" (96.5 x 96.5cm)

The Duchess of Dirt

This porcine photo was taken while I was on an artists' residency in the Bahamas. The pig lived on the farm of the school that hosted me. This is the first quilt in which I used a one-color background. As soon as I started piecing it together, I knew I would continue to explore that technique for the rest of the quilts. The cohesiveness of a color wash pushes each animal into the foreground and highlights their individuality.

Finished quilt size 37" x 37" (94 x 94cm)

The Empress of Ewes

Curls are seductive. The sheep's wool drew me in, and I wanted to replicate every ringlet. That was certainly not feasible, so I had to pick and choose a few representative curls to make. After the quilt was finished and bound, I found there was not enough definition between the ewe's face and her body. To add depth and definition, I went back in and added curlicue quilting stitches to her face with a dark thread. Just that bit of shading was what the quilt needed.

Finished quilt size 38" x 38" (96.5 x 96.5cm)

Individual Portraits

The following four quilts were created as standalone pieces and each has a distinctive style. *The Brown Chicken* quilt on page 96, in particular, showcases how stitched mosaic quilting can be just as effective in a small size with simpler fabrics.

Daisy the Corgi

You do not need to make a large quilt to create an adorable portrait! I used my home printer to print the photo of Daisy onto a single piece of letter-sized paper. The added borders make the quilt slightly bigger, but still a very

Finished quilt size 11½" x 14" (29.2 x 35.6cm)

I Woke Up Like This

This is a self-portrait of my morning hair. I think of myself as having strawberry blonde hair, but as I worked on this quilt, I realized my hair is more of a "William Morris Brown," as my William Morris collection of fabrics matched my hair perfectly. The organic shapes and the variety of colors in the fabrics mimic the shapes and color variety in my hair.

Finished quilt size 47" x 47" (1.2 x 1.2m)

Brown Chicken

This chicken was originally intended for *Zooming Chickens* but did not make it into the larger quilt. I decided to turn it into a quick, small wall hanging using buttons for the eyes.

Finished quilt size 8" x 8" (20.3 x 20.3cm)

Zooming Chickens

This quilt is made from twenty different photographs, each printed on 8½" x 11" (21.6 x 27.9cm) paper on my home printer. I made each chicken as its own block, then sewed the blocks together to create a larger piece. Originally this quilt was titled *The Broody Bunch*, but after we all spent 2020 on our computers looking at each other in little boxes, *Zooming Chickens* seemed like a more appropriate title.

For this chicken, I used the same photo that I used for *Charming Chicken* on page 89. Since the scale was smaller here, I included fewer details.

Finished quilt size 33" x 41" (83.8cm x 1m)

Comparing this finished block to the original inspiration demonstrates how complex shapes can be edited to convey only the most important information.

The eye in the original inspiration photo had a lot of personality, and the finished block shows how catchlights in the eye can bring that life and personality to a stitched mosaic subject.

Early Works

Every quilt we make is a learning experience and steppingstone to our next project. The quilts below each taught me something that set me on the path toward creating the stitched mosaic process (even though I had no idea at the time where I was headed).

O Happy Day

O Happy Day was a breakthrough for me and how I think about arranging color. I made 300+ circle-on-square blocks without much of a plan, and then had to think about how to organize them into a quilt. Each layout I tried was overwhelming due to all the different options spinning in my head. How did that block look next to this one? Should an orange circle sit next to another orange circle? How do I make it cohesive and not just a big scrappy jumble? Finally, I narrowed my decision process down to one variable: the background color. This quilt, and many of the quilts I have made since then, are laid out by only looking at the background of each block. In this case I ignored the color of the foreground circles and just considered the color of the squares to determine block placement. *O Happy Day* taught me how to make a color wash across a quilt, and how to truly use value as a major design element.

Finished quilt size: 70" x 66" (1.8 x 1.7m)

On the Fly

Like *O Happy Day*, the body of this quilt was laid out using the background—the fabrics in the corners and center of each block. In *On the Fly*, you can see how scraps can be used to create an effective border design. Because I only buy small amounts of yardage, I usually do not have enough of any one fabric for a border. Instead of going to the store, I pieced these borders using many different fabrics from my stash to create a color wash around the quilt. The variation in colors and values within the border makes it more interesting than it would be with just one or two fabrics.

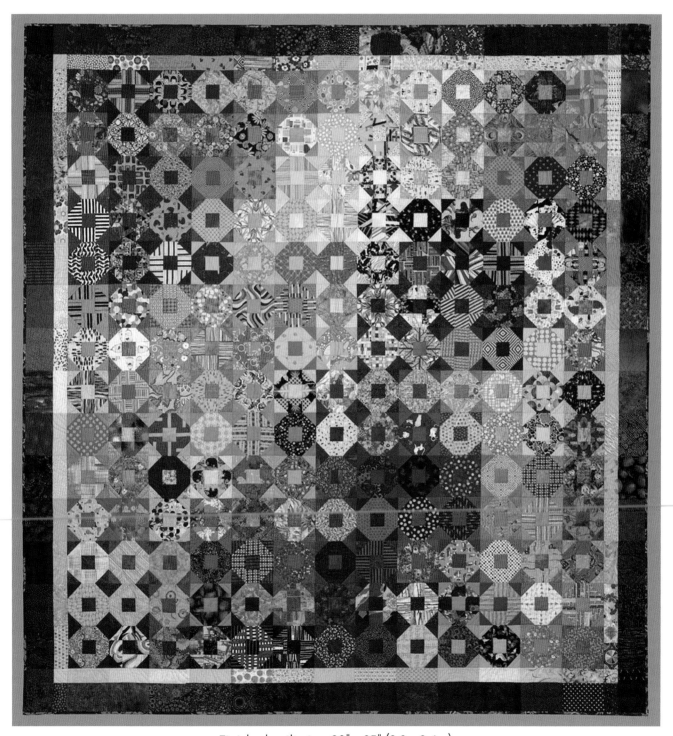

Finished quilt size: 89" x 95" (2.3 x 2.4m)

Catena

Most of the quilts I make have a rule to get me started. This one's rule was "pink and green," a favorite complementary color combination of mine (see the *Cheeky Cat* project on page 85 and the *Rhubarb Leaf* project on page 70, which both mix pink and green touches). Once I ran out of true pinks and greens from my stash, I expanded my definition of pink and green. Looking at the color wheel showed me how pink often bleeds into reds and oranges, while green moves into blues and yellows. I make the rules, so I can expand and change them as needed!

Finished quilt size: 67" x 62" (1.7 x 1.6m)

Mass Maples

Mass Maples is my New England autumn quilt. My color rule was to use real colors that I see in October: autumnal leaf colors for the leaves, and fall sky, bark, and grass colors for the backgrounds. The maple leaf blocks are set on point to create strong, dynamic diagonals. This, along with the wide variety of values within the quilt, gives the impression of the leaves dancing as they fall. Similarly, I always set my stitched mosaic quilts on point as it immediately helps the viewer's eye move across the quilt.

Finished quilt size: 74" x 80" (1.9 x 2m)

Flicker

While this string quilt is made up of blocks sewn together in straight rows, the diagonals within each block give the design movement and energy. Scrappy string quilts are also my favorite way to experiment and play with color combinations. They are easy to make, and they always look great!

Finished quilt size: 52" x 52" (1.3 x 1.3m)

Holyoke 1938

Holyoke 1938 was the first map quilt I made, and it really pushed me to expand my work beyond block-based quilts. To get started, I had the map printed to 24" x 36" (61 x 91.4cm) and used the paper map as a pattern. Enlarging images became a simple, but crucial, part of how I work. Notice how I (unintentionally) used complementary colors (blue and orange) for the major elements within the finished quilt.

The enlarged map was my main inspiration for this piece, but I kept the smaller original map and other maps of the area nearby to use as references while I worked.

I unintentionally chose complementary colors for the water and street grids, but you can see from my sketching on the background fabric that I was very intentional about how I added these elements.

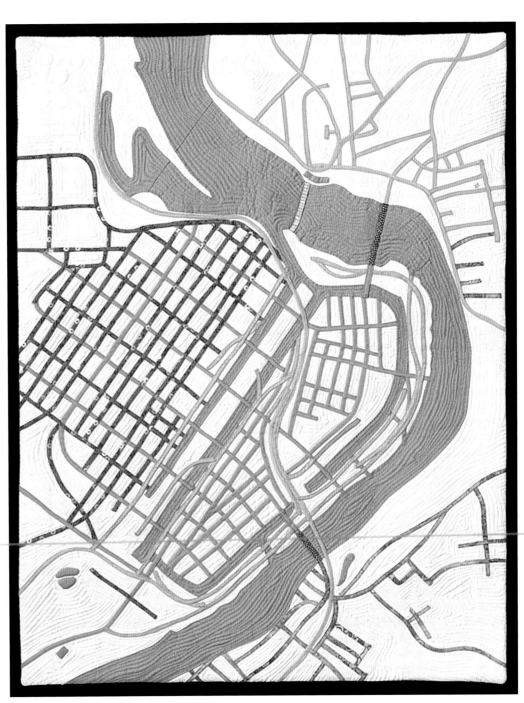

Finished quilt size: 22" x 29" (55.9 x 73.7cm)

Roses in the Rotary

This is a map quilt of the neighborhood I lived in when I made it. Each piece is appliquéd onto a white background. The white that shows through represents the streets, while the colorful pieces are city "blocks." The blue ombré represents the Connecticut River, which in reality is more of a mossy green color. While the seam lines in stitched mosaic projects act as the "mortar" between the mosaic pieces, here the white streets serve that purpose.

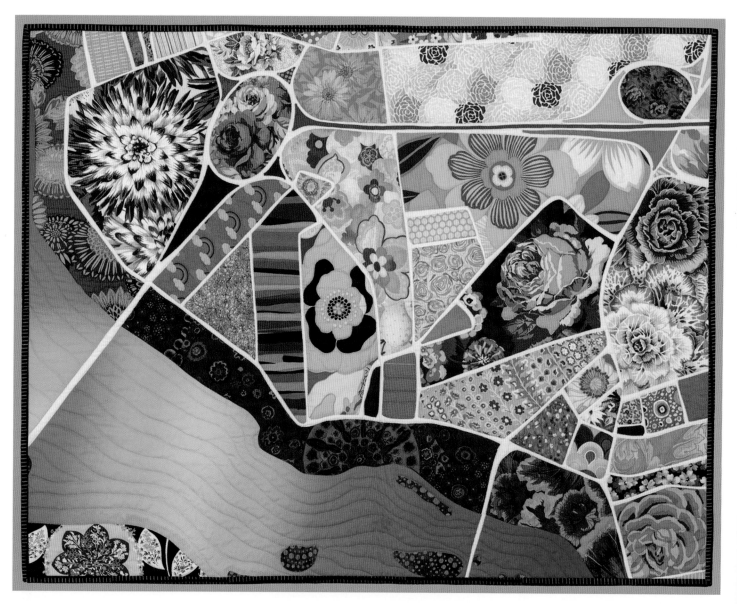

Finished quilt size: 36" x 28" (91.4 x 71.1cm)

Mississippi Meander

This map depicts a 10-mile stretch of the Mississippi River between Arkansas and Mississippi, based on a drawn by the Army Corp of Engineers. To make this map quilt, I enlarged the original map to the finished quilt, then broke down the construction process into smaller pieces. In this case, I made one oxbow at a ti sewed the oxbows together. I also built the quilt right on top of the image, a technique I now use to constr stitched mosaic pieces.

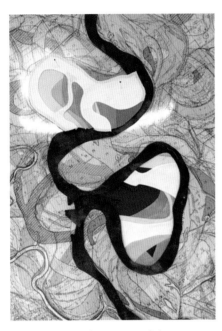

Working directly on top of the enlarged map allowed me to create each oxbow as a small piece and gradually build them all together, using the actual inspirational image as a guide.

Finished quilt size: 44" x 66" (1.1 x 1.7m)

How to Use This Book

This is a guidebook. While there are patterns, photos, and practice projects included, my goal is to lay out the steps of the stitched mosaic technique so that you can take my ideas and make quilts that are unique to you. After all, the most meaningful quilts are those with stories behind them and those made for the people we love.

I do recommend that you read through all the chapters before starting on your first stitched mosaic quilt. There are tips and tricks sprinkled throughout the book that will help you through the process from start to finish.

Explore the basic tools and get started in Chapter 1, then investigate ways to think about color in Chapter 2. The basic construction techniques are covered in Chapter 3, beginning on page 58, where I will walk you through creating the *Blue Daisy* design. This is the foundation that will help you get started on your own stitched mosaic quilt journey. As you run into problems or tricky blocks, you will want to check out the troubleshooting tips in Chapter 4. Begin by making the *Blue Daisy* design, then try out one or more of the projects in Chapter 5 to familiarize yourself with the process. Once you are ready to move on to a larger or more meaningful project, take the tools and knowledge gained in these first few practice pieces and apply them to the image and quilt that speaks to your heart.

The projects are presented in order of difficulty from the smallest and simplest to the largest and most complex. All seam allowances are ¼" (6.4mm) unless otherwise specified.

Remember, if you make one of my patterns, feel free to change the colors, the size, or whatever feels right to you. My Grandma Ortha always said that recipes and quilt patterns are just suggestions. Go forth and make this your own!

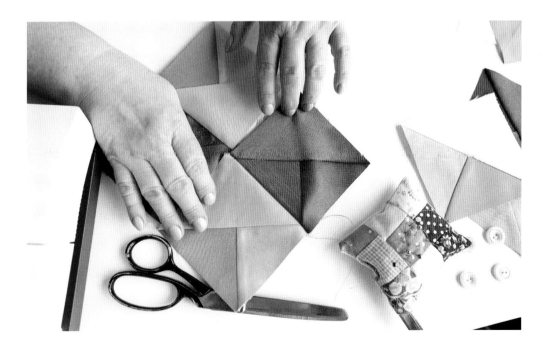

CHAPTER 1:
Getting Started

General Supplies

Many of the supplies needed to make a stitched mosaic quilt are the same tools needed to make traditional quilts. Some basic sewing supplies required include a rotary cutter, cutting mat, rulers, seam ripper, iron, and ironing board. If you are already a quilter, you will probably have these supplies on hand.

The items below include a few things that you will need for this technique that may not be on a "basic sewing supplies" list and recommendations and guidelines for using the items you might already have.

Printed photo—Every stitched mosaic quilt starts with a photo. The photo then becomes the base for the pattern. This photo needs to be blown up to the finished size of the quilt. See pages 35–40 for more information on choosing and printing a photo.

Freezer paper—Freezer paper is my favorite quilting tool, although you won't find it in quilt shops. Look for it in grocery stores and big box department stores. It is usually stocked with plastic wrap and aluminum foil. Freezer paper has a shiny side and a dull side. The shiny side  has a wax or plastic coating on it designed to keep food protected while it is in the freezer. Quilters discovered that the shiny side melts slightly when ironed, allowing the paper to stick to fabric without leaving a residue when it is removed. Freezer paper is especially helpful for making appliqué templates, which is exactly what it is used for in the stitched mosaic technique. You will need to cut your freezer paper into 2" (5.1cm) squares using a rotary cutter and a blade designed to cut paper. Die cutting machines with 2" square dies and laser cutters can also be used to cut the paper into squares.

Light-colored ultra fine point permanent marker—I use a light-colored Ultra Fine Point Sharpie to draw on my freezer paper templates. You really do need a light marker (try orange, light green, or light blue) with a very fine point for this task. If your markings get wet, they may bleed slightly. Using a light color keeps this bleeding from being visible on your quilt.

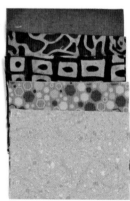

Scraps of fabric cut into 2½" (6.4cm) squares—You will need a wide variety of colors and values that correspond with the palette of your photo. If you already have a scrap bin, dig through it to find some of the colors you need before cutting into your stash. Ask quilting friends to contribute to your project if you are looking for a specific color. Many of us are happy to share, since scraps seem to breed no matter how many quilts we make.

Black fine point permanent marker—I usually use a black Fine Point Sharpie®, often called a "regular" Sharpie, for drawing a grid on top of my inspiration photo. The marker you use doesn't need to have a particularly narrow point; it just needs to be a good size for drawing your grid.

Small paint brush—My favorite is a ¼" (6.4mm) angled brush purchased for a couple of dollars from my local art supply store. I use this brush to paint starch or starch alternatives on the seam allowances around the templates.

Your favorite liquid starch—Starch and starch alternatives are used for two purposes. The first is to moisten fabric so that it is malleable and will wrap around the freezer paper templates with ease. The second is that we want the seam allowances (the extra fabric edge surrounding our appliqué pieces) to stay folded over in place while we work. Once the fabric is dried with an iron, the starch holds the crease and keeps the seam allowances exactly where we want them. Throughout this book, I will use the terms starch and starch alternative interchangeably. I often use Mary Ellen's Best Press™, but use the product you prefer.

Small, shallow bowl—Used to hold liquid starch or starch alternatives.

Scrap of cotton batting—About 4" x 6" (10.2 x 15.2cm). Used as a blotter to absorb extra liquid when it is being painted on the fabric.

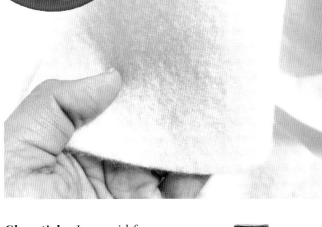

Glue stick—I use acid-free, washable glue sticks because I like to know that the glue will dissolve when I wash the quilt, or, if I do not wash the quilt, that the glue will not hurt the fabric. Glue sticks that smear on as purple and dry clear are my favorites. They are readily available at office supply and big box stores. Glue pens designed for quilters are another option. They have smaller tips for more targeted application.

Quilting rulers in various sizes—A 6" x 24" (15.2 x 61cm) ruler with a 45-degree line printed on it is a handy size to have. For drawing long lines, you may need to tape a few rulers together. I usually use my 6½" (16.5cm) square ruler for cutting the 2½" (6.4cm) squares.

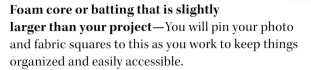

Scissors, for fabric and paper—My favorite scissors are Karen Kay Buckley 6" Perfect Scissors™. They have a fine serrated edge that grips the fabric when cutting, and any similar fabric scissors will do the job. I confess I usually break the cardinal quilting rule of keeping paper away from fabric scissors. I use my fabric scissors to cut freezer paper because I usually can't be bothered to swap out scissors as I work. You have my permission to use your scissors however you wish.

Foam core or batting that is slightly larger than your project—You will pin your photo and fabric squares to this as you work to keep things organized and easily accessible.

Quilter's Moonshine

Recently, while teaching a class, some participants shared a homemade starch recipe with me that they referred to as "quilter's moonshine." When I did an internet search, I found many different recipes, but most include mixing the following ingredients together and pouring into spray bottles:

- 1 gallon distilled water
- ½ cup liquid starch
- 1 cup cheap vodka

It's an inexpensive, easy starch alternative to make. And it works great!

Small trash bin—The stitched mosaic process makes a huge mess of little pieces of paper and fabric. I always have a small tabletop bin nearby so I can throw out scraps as soon as I am finished with them.

Sewing machine—I recommend a machine that can do a zigzag or blanket stitch, but that feature, while helpful, is not required.

Straight pins—For the projects in this book, you probably have enough pins on hand. Large projects require many more pins than I can usually find in my sewing space. If you work on a large scale, you may need additional straight pins. My favorite pins are Clover Art No. 232 Patchwork Pins, which have iron-proof glass heads and a 0.5mm diameter shaft that is 36mm long.

Stiletto—Also referred to as sewing stilettos or laying tools, these are handy for manipulating fabric while machine appliquéing, but aren't necessary. Anything long and pointy will work—a chopstick or bamboo skewer, the pointy end of a seam ripper, scissors, or even a long straight pin.

Double-sided fusible interfacing—Double-sided fusible interfacing is helpful but not necessary. While many portrait and mosaic quilts rely heavily on double-sided fusible interfacing, I use it only occasionally in stitched mosaic pieces. It is very helpful for tiny pieces like the catchlights in eyes. HeatnBond®, Steam-A-Seam 2®, Wonder-Under®, and Mistyfuse® are popular brands.

Iron—Irons are indispensable in helping fabrics to adhere together during the appliqué process and for pressing seams and finishing.

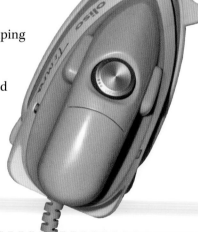

Light box—This is helpful for tracing. I find that I use the light box when I am working on small projects, like the ones in this book. For larger projects, I find the photos to be too cumbersome to move around, so the light box does not get used.

TIP: I keep two sewing machines set up in my studio. One is loaded with clear monofilament thread and is always ready to blanket stitch. The second machine is threaded with cotton thread to piece blocks together. By keeping the tasks for each machine separate, I do not need to change threads when I move from appliqué to piecing. I know this setup is not feasible for everyone, but it was a game changer for me when I realized I could do this.

Tools for Machine Appliqué

Along with the general supplies previously listed, a few small tools and accessories will make a huge difference when machine appliquéing.

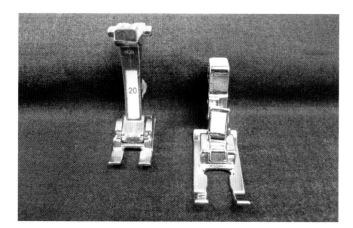

The large open area on open toe embroidery feet allows for greater visibility that will help with machine appliquéing the smaller details in mosaic quilts.

Open Toe Embroidery Foot—While not necessary, an open toe embroidery foot is helpful. This foot allows plenty of visibility so that you can really see where you are sewing. If you do not have an open toe foot, use a zigzag or reverse pattern foot (these usually come with the machine). Clear feet are especially helpful.

Top thread for appliqué—My thread of choice for machine appliqué is clear monofilament thread, like MonoPoly™ thread by Superior® Threads, because I do not want the appliqué threads to be visible on my pieces. Monofilament thread is my BFF (best friend forever). It hides my mistakes and makes my life easier. I like to sew fast, and sometimes that means that I veer off course, but when the thread is invisible, the casual observer will never know of my lead-foot tendencies. I also like that clear thread always matches whatever I am working on. I can stitch down many different fabric colors in one sitting without having to change my thread colors. When using clear thread in the top of the machine, do not use it in the bobbin. I thread the invisible thread through the top of my sewing machine and use a 50 wt. cotton or poly thread in the bobbin.

Monofilament threads have come a long way in 20 years. I hated sewing with the nylon threads of the early 2000s—they stretched and broke and were generally miserable to work with. Fortunately, there are several good clear polyester threads on the market now. Use a thread that runs well through your sewing machine and can be ironed over with the highest heat of an iron and machine washed and dried. Every sewing machine (and every user's tolerance) is different, so use the thread that

works best for you and your machine. If you do not want to use an invisible thread, choose threads that generally match your project. The thread should match the top appliqué piece rather than the base layer.

Clear monofilament thread is the best top thread to use for appliqué in your stitched mosaic projects, especially if you are learning the process, since any small mistakes will be be hidden.

Bobbin Thread—When using monofilament thread in the top of the machine, use a thin cotton or polyester thread in a neutral color in the bobbin. I usually use something like a gray or beige 50 wt. 100% cotton Aurifil thread or a 60 wt. polyester Superior Threads Bottom Line thread in the bobbin. When not using a monofilament thread, I use the same thread in both the top and bobbin of my machine.

Your choice of needle will probably change based on the machine you're using and the thread you prefer, but I tend to stick with Superior Threads Titanium Coated Topstitch 80/12 needles for general piecing and appliqué.

Needles—Many quilters have strong feelings about needles. I do not. If I am doing general piecing or appliqué, I almost always use Superior Threads Titanium Coated Topstitch 80/12 needles for use with 50 wt. thread. Occasionally, if I can see the needle holes in my appliqué pieces, I change to a smaller needle, usually size 70/10. Again, your choice may vary depending

Working with Monofilament Thread

Monofilament thread can take a little getting used to. If you've never used it before, keep the following tips in mind to make the transition smoother:

- Always loosen the top tension on your sewing machine when using clear thread. On my Bernina, I set the tensioner to a 2, rather than its neutral position at 4. On my Juki, I turn the tensioner dial counterclockwise at least one full revolution. Test different tensions while you practice to find the one that works best for you.

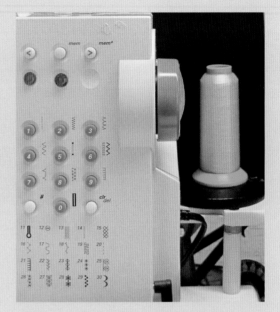

- Sometimes the bobbin tension may need to be tightened slightly. *Note: this cannot be done if you have a drop-in bobbin.* If your bobbin case has a pigtail, pull the thread through the small hole at the end of the pigtail. This puts a little resistance on the bobbin thread, which helps pull the top thread to the back of the block, so it is invisible on top.

- Use the vertical spool holder if your machine has one.

- When using a cone, put it on a thread stand. Thread stands can be flimsy, though. Look for one with a metal base.

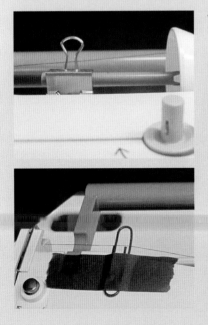

- If your machine only has a horizontal thread holder, you may need to improvise an additional guide or two for the thread to travel through before it goes through the prescribed path. These guides may help control the thread after it comes off the spool. Attach a binder clip or use painter's tape to tape a paper clip to the top of the sewing machine. The clips should be between the thread spool and the first thread guide on the machine.

- If you don't have a thread stand, place the spool in a coffee mug, then thread through the machine (use added paper clip guides if needed). The cup will help keep the cone from bouncing around while allowing the thread to come off the top of the cone.

Choosing a Photo

Every stitched mosaic piece starts with a photograph. Choosing a photo to work from is your first important design decision to make. The photo starts as the inspiration. After it is printed, it becomes the pattern.

Some images immediately grab your attention. These types of images can be the best starting points for stitched mosaic quilts.

A photo that is visually striking on its own will make a spectacular quilt easier to achieve since the underlying design is already well established. I made some of my quilts, like *Up Close and Personal* (page 7) and *The Duchess of Dirt* (page 14), because the original photos were strong images that I wanted to recreate. Other quilts only came about after I took dozens of photos of the same subject, trying to snap the "perfect" shot. This happens most frequently when I am trying to get my cat, Thumper (the inspiration for the *Cheeky Cat* project on page 85), to look at the camera. She is crafty and knows how to look away just as I press the shutter button!

Many photos hold memories. Photos of beloved pets and adorable grandchildren are popular subjects with students in my classes. In these instances, try to find a photo that captures the character of the subject. Maybe it is the way they cock their head, or how their grin shows off a missing front tooth after a visit from the tooth fairy. If the photo captures the essence of the subject, the quilt will do the same.

Rarely will you have a "perfect" photo to work from. Backgrounds need to be edited out and items such as fences and random arms should be ignored (see the photos below; compare the *Dashing Dog* inspiration photo with the finished quilt). When I am working, I only focus on recreating the main subject, and then I replace everything behind it with a color wash in the background. The photo may be the roadmap, but you can take a detour into artistic license any time you like.

TIP: You do not need a fancy camera to take pictures that work for this technique. I use my iPhone for almost all my stitched mosaic quilt reference photos. The phone takes decent photos, and I always have it in my pocket, so it is easy to spontaneously photograph something as it strikes me. If you decide to use an older printed photo or a photo that was taken with an older digital camera, be aware that when the photo is printed at a larger size, the image may become fuzzy and pixelated.

Some photos require editing to create a perfect stitched mosaic quilt arrangement. The inspiration photo for the *Dashing Dog* project captures the dog's personality but also includes arms in the background that would detract from the composition if included in the final quilt.

Photograph Guidelines

Your main subject should fill the frame of your reference photo. While you do want to have some background visible, the most important element should take up most of the space. It is also helpful if the main image has clear, defined edges. Rather than taking a photo of a whole garden, consider zooming in and shooting a close-up shot of one flower. I have found photos where the main image fills the frame produce more striking results than photos that are less specific to the subject.

    Use a well-lit photo. Make sure that you can see the color and variation of shapes within the photo.

Compare the full garden photo on the left with the other two photos that focus on individual flowers. For creating a stitched mosaic quilt, having one well-defined subject in your photo will create more stunning results.

The photo of the chicken on the left is much too dark and unfocused to use for a stitched mosaic quilt. The zoomed-in photo on the right is brighter and better frames the subject.

Try to be at eye level with the subject. The strength of the subject comes through when it is looking straight at you. Photos taken from above the subject have a less powerful visual impact than those taken at or below eye level. Sometimes I need to take dozens of photos to get the "right" picture. Don't be afraid to snap and delete.

Cropping can be your friend. If an image doesn't fill the frame in a way that you like, crop the photo so that less background shows. You can do this using photo editing software, or just cut off the excess after the photo is printed.

Here is the final cropped version I would use as the template for my stitched mosaic quilt.

This original photo of Sarge the dog includes too much background for my purposes.

Be respectful of copyright. Use images that you have taken yourself, have permission to use, or images that are copyright free. There is a lot of gray area regarding fair use and copyright laws, so, to be safe, I only use images that fit in the above categories. If you find an image created by someone else that you wish to use, send a friendly inquiry to the owner of that image asking if you can use it to make an art quilt. In my experience, people are excited to see how artists will interpret their work. But if they do not grant you permission to use it, move on to another photograph.

The daisy I used as the template for the *Blue Daisy* project on page 58 was photographed by my good friend, Jennifer Ewers. Jennifer is generously allowing you to use her image in learning the stitched mosaic techniques. Please

A Note about United States Copyright Law

As of 2022, many images produced in 1926 or earlier are in the public domain, since it is more than 95 years since the first publication date, but you should always confirm that with the copyright holder. Photographs, maps, and other visuals produced by the U.S. federal government are often copyright free. The Library of Congress is a tremendous resource that has a link to "free-to-use" images on their website. It's always fun to poke around and be inspired by the images they have available. See *https://www.loc.gov/free-to-use/*

Many other large libraries and institutions have images available for use. They are found within collections on their website. The key phrases to look for on each image are "free to use without restriction" or "no known copyright restrictions."

Preparing the Photo

Once you have decided which photo you want to replicate, the next step is preparing the photo: having it blown up and printed at the finished size of the quilt and drawing your grid. Your reference image needs to be printed at the size of the finished quilt so that you can use the printed photo as the pattern for the quilt.

Printing the Photo

For printing, the reference photo needs to be a JPEG or PDF digital file. The larger the file, the better the print quality, but I have found that a JPEG sent from my phone is more than large enough to print at 40" (1m) square. The goal is to get a decent print to work from. For this purpose, it does not necessarily need to be high quality.

If you use an older photo that has been in a frame or photo album, you will need to scan it and save it as a digital file. Scanning and formatting are services that most copy shops provide if you need assistance turning your image into a digital file. Another option is to use one of the many phone scanner apps available in app stores. These apps use your phone's camera to take a picture and convert the document to a PDF or JPEG.

For most of us, blowing up the photo and having it printed "large format" requires going to a professional copy shop. Many shops can print up to 48" (1.2m) wide

and any length, but every printer has different parameters. Ask your local shop what they can provide. I order my photos to be printed at a specific length or width, whichever is more important to me for the project. The other measurement is determined by the proportion of the photo. Keep in mind that quilts shrink a bit as they are quilted and trimmed, so the finished quilt will probably be a bit smaller than the printed photo. I have made several quilts where the photos are printed at 40" x 40" (1 x 1m) and the finished quilts are 37" (94cm) square.

Have the photo printed on the cheapest paper that is offered. Printing on this paper may lead to duller colors than having the photo printed on a high-quality paper, but that is ok. The photo is your pattern, not the finished product. You will mark up the printed image, make

Where and How to Get Your Photo Printed

There are several options for where and how to have oversize prints made ("oversize" just means larger than legal size paper, which is 8½" x 14" [21.6 x 35.6cm]). The options below are listed in order of my preference but use the method that works best for you and your circumstances.

Local, independent copy shops—I love using my local shops because they have great customer service and are always helpful when I have questions. If I tell them what I am looking for, they recommend the best paper and printing process for my needs.

Big box office supply stores—Often you need to order the prints through their websites. Large prints are listed under "oversize print," "large format," "posters," etc. In my experience, the websites are not very flexible. If you are unsure of what you need, and you can call ahead or stop into the store to speak with someone in customer service, that is always the best option. The salespeople know the products and will help you get on the right track.

Home printer—There are two options for printing at home. Some websites will help you figure out how to print out the enlarged photo on multiple sheets of 8½" x 11" (21.6 x 27.9cm) copy paper. You can then tape those pages together to complete the photo. I've successfully used *https://www.blockposters.com*, but a quick internet search for "block posters" will turn up many useful websites you can use. A similar technique can be achieved using Microsoft Excel. Insert your photo into cell A1 of a new spreadsheet. Then view the image in Page Layout to get an idea of the number of pages the image will print on. If you need to make the image larger, click on the corner of the image box while holding the shift key. Expand the image by holding down the shift key and dragging the bottom right corner of the image. Once the image is the size you want, print it out on multiple pages and tape them together.

Drawing the Grid

Now that you have a large, printed photo, you need to draw a grid on top of it with your black fine point marker. This is also the time to decide which way is up in the picture. Sometimes it is obvious, especially if your photo is of a person or animal, but other images are less clear. I often get confused with flowers, so I write "TOP" at the top of the photo. It is a quick thing to do that keeps me organized.

Square Photo Grids

Creating a grid over a square photo is a very straightforward process. With square photos you can conveniently achieve a perfect 45-degree angle for your starting line by drawing from corner to corner.

1. Draw a diagonal line from the upper left corner to the bottom right corner. This line will create a 45-degree angle through the photo. Make sure that the point of the marker starts exactly in the top left corner and ends exactly in the bottom right corner. Your ruler will sit just slightly to the left of the corner to compensate for the width of the marker tip. In these photos, I'm showing how I draw the lines as a right-handed person. If your left hand is

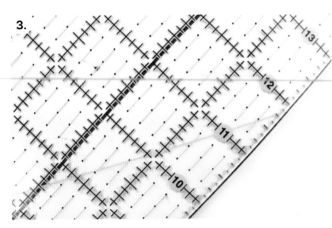

2. Draw a second diagonal line from the upper right corner and the bottom left corner. It is important that the second line is **perpendicular** to the first line. If you use a quilter's ruler to draw the lines, this angle is easy to check. Two sides of one of the squares printed on the ruler will line up with the two drawn lines on the paper.

4. As you work, keep an eye on your line intersections. They should always create right angles.

3. Draw a 2" (5.1 cm) grid across the rest of the photo. To get accurate 2" squares, you need to account for the width of the marker line when drawing subsequent grid lines. I accommodate for this by placing the 2" line of my ruler just to the left of the drawn line rather than exactly on top of it. Let the ruler line ride along next to the marked line. If you are left-handed, you'll place the 2" ruler line just to the right of the drawn line.

TIP: Once your photo is gridded, number the squares (see the photo above). This will keep you organized while you work. It is easier to remember you are working on square number 26, rather than the square that is "over here, kind of in the middle." I made many quilts using the "over here, kind of in the middle" technique, but you should save yourself some time and aggravation by labeling your squares.

Rectangular Photo Grids

Rectangular photos are a bit trickier than square ones. With rectangular photos, you focus only on drawing 45-degree lines from the top two corners, ignoring the bottom two corners.

TIP: Place a piece of painter's tape or washi tape along the 45-degree line on your ruler to make it more visible when making your first lines.

2. Repeat step 1, this time starting from the upper right corner. Make sure that the two lines are perpendicular and make a 90-degree angle where they intersect. Having a right angle there is key to ensuring that the grid is composed of squares, rather than rhombuses.

1. Place your quilter's ruler in the top left corner of the photo and line up the 45-degree angle line on your ruler with the left edge of the photograph. Draw the line with your black fine point marker diagonally across the photo.

Making a Long Ruler for Larger Projects

If the printed photo is bigger than 18" (45.7cm), a standard 6" x 24" (15.2 x 61cm) quilter's ruler will not be long enough to draw lines across the whole photo. To make an extra-long straight edge, I tape several rulers together using blue painter's tape. As long as one edge is long and smooth, you can get accurate measurements all the way across the photo. I draw the longest lines first—those closest to the first two intersecting lines. As I move out toward the edge of the photo, I remove the extra rulers as they are no longer needed.

3. Draw a 2" (5.1cm) grid over the rest of the photo. See Square Photo Grids step 3 on page 41 and the Tip on page

A Few Notes on the Grid Structure

Why is the grid made up of 2" (5.1cm) squares?
Honestly, 2" was an arbitrary measurement I decided on when I made my first stitched mosaic piece. I had a pile of 2½" (6.4cm) squares I wanted to incorporate that would finish at 2" when they were sewn together and 2½" is a common measurement in the quilting world. Jelly rolls are cut that width, and manufacturers sell 2½" squares in mini charm packs. Now I make all my stitched mosaics with a 2" grid because I already have boxes full of 2½" squares cut and ready to go into my next project.

While the projects in this book are all based on a 2" (5.1cm) grid, there is absolutely no reason you need to draw your grid that size. If 3" (7.6cm) feels better for you, go for it. If 5" (12.7cm) seems like a good idea, try it! Just remember that your fabric squares need to be cut to ½" (1.3cm) bigger than your drawn grid.

Why is the grid diagonal, and can I make mine a straight grid? First, you can absolutely make your quilt using a straight grid. All the construction steps would

be the same as for a diagonal grid. The only difference is the direction in which the lines are drawn.

There are two reasons why I draw lines on the diagonal. The first is aesthetic. I always like quilts that are set with the blocks on-point. Strong diagonals make for visually dynamic quilts, as the angled seam lines help the viewer's eye move across the quilt. Quilts made with this technique are visually pleasing since the diagonals are based on 45-degree and 90-degree angles. If we changed the angles of the blocks, the piece might become more visually unsettling—and be harder to piece together.

The practical reason I work on the diagonal does not come into play until the quilt is almost finished. When trimming a quilt down after it is quilted, sometimes I find that my seam lines have shifted, or they aren't exactly as square or straight as I would like them to be. With trim lines that are parallel and perpendicular to the seam lines, any discrepancy or wobbly seam lines are obvious. If the quilt is pieced on the diagonal, then

TIP: Rubbing alcohol removes Sharpie marks from rulers. I keep alcohol prep pads in my studio for easy clean up.

CHAPTER 2:
Color and Fabric Choices

A successful stitched mosaic piece is not only about the structure, but it also uses color and fabric in ways that highlight the primary image. I know that the process of planning out colors is intimidating for some quilters, so I encourage those people to play and have fun. There are no "right" or "wrong" ways to put together your project. This section illustrates how I think about color and what I am looking for when designing a quilt, and I hope it will help you discover your favorite color style as well!

Make Color Rules You Can Work With

Every quilt I make starts with a "rule." Often it is a color rule that allows me to work within some parameters and not feel overwhelmed by the sheer number of options available to me. That is why most of my stitched mosaic quilts have one-color backgrounds. I consider the background to be anything behind the main figure. I want the background to have some movement and interest, but not detract from the main focal point.

If I make the rule "use only blue-green in the background," like I did in *The Duchess of Dirt* on page 14, I do not need to pull out my bins of red or orange fabrics and consider them. I already know that they are not options. And any time I need to change the rule, I can. After all, it's my own rule I am breaking!

Even though I say that my stitched mosaic quilts have one-color backgrounds, they really have many different hues, patterns, and values within them. That variety is what gives the backgrounds movement and visual texture. Using *The Duchess of Dirt* as an example again, while I am trying to use only "blue-green" fabric, my definition of blue-green is expansive. I use colors that blue-green bleeds into along the color wheel (see page 46) and a variety of lights and darks within those colors.

The Duchess of Dirt quilt demonstrates my use of a color rule (using a single color for the background), but also shows the variation in pattern, hue, and value that is still possible within a color rule.

The same concept applies to the main figures themselves. I worked within a "purple" color rule for the main flower in the *Bearded Iris* project on page 99, and, while some of the fabrics are more blue-purple and some are quite light in value, they all fit into my rule for the finished quilt.

An exception to the one-color background is *The Marquess of Muscovy* on page 12. For this duck, rather than set a color rule, I set a pattern rule: to use floral fabrics. I cut 2½" (6.4cm) squares out of all the floral fabrics in my stash and then arranged them in an order reminiscent of a rainbow.

TIP: How do I know which color rule to choose for a quilt background? My goal is for the figure in my stitched mosaic piece to pop off the background, so I often use a color that is complementary to the image. For the *Bearded Iris* project on page 99, I chose a yellow background because I knew it would look great with its complementary color, purple.

Use Colors That Make You Happy

I like bright, clear colors and I enjoy the challenge of putting many colors together. My color combinations can be "too much" for some people and that is ok with me. Color is tied to our emotions and past experiences, so what makes me happy color-wise is not necessarily what works for you. Part of the fun of playing with color and fabric is figuring out what combinations speak to our own personal aesthetics.

Use Color to Keep Yourself Organized

The organizational systems in my house and studio are color coded because that is how my brain works. I use colored file folders on my desk. Green folders hold bank statements and credit card receipts, while red folders hold notes for long-term projects.

My fabric is stored in bins sorted by color. There are one or two bins per color, and separate bins for solids and novelties. The bins titled "neutrals" are catch-alls of beiges, grays, and browns. "Neutrals" are not my favorite colors, but they are needed to enhance the bright pops of color I love.

My scrap bins are also sorted into color families. Reds, oranges, and yellows are in one bin; greens, blues, and purples are in a second bin; and neutrals are in a third bin. Since I began making stitched mosaic quilts, I have also accumulated a stash of 2½" (6.4cm) squares. These squares are sorted into shoebox-size bins, again grouped by color families like my larger scrap bins.

Color Confidence Can Be Learned

People often tell me that I have a good color sense. Guess what? That was not always the case, and I have plenty of not-so-pretty quilts to prove it. I believe that most people learn how to use color through experience. Playing with fabric and trying out color combinations has taught me how to really look at color and how to use it effectively. Also with practice, I now know what color combinations I like together, and I tend to use them over and over.

I spent 15 years as a longarm quilter. That experience taught me as much about color as it did about quilting. Every day, I chose threads to match or contrast with the quilt tops I was being hired to quilt. That daily practice trained my eye to be able to choose the right thread for the project quickly. My clients also taught me to be open to new combinations. Sometimes, a client would come in with a specific thread color idea and I would have my doubts. When the color turned out to be perfect, it was a huge lesson for me to experiment with unexpected alternatives.

Trying out new or bold color combinations in a large quilt can be intimidating due to the amount of time and money that goes into making a quilt. Quilters often choose the "safe" option and pick colors that we know go together because we do not want to "waste" fabric or time. Try out new color combinations on small projects—make a postcard or potholder, or just sew some fabrics together with no expectations. If you do not like the result, toss out the experiment and think of the time and fabric used as an investment in your quilting education. Experimenting, making bold choices, and sometimes failing are all part of the process when gaining color

Using the Color Wheel

Color wheels can tell you an immense amount of information about the theory of color. I find that the amount of information provided can be overwhelming, so I use the wheel as a tool to help me solve immediate problems by finding analogous and complementary colors and other shade variations.

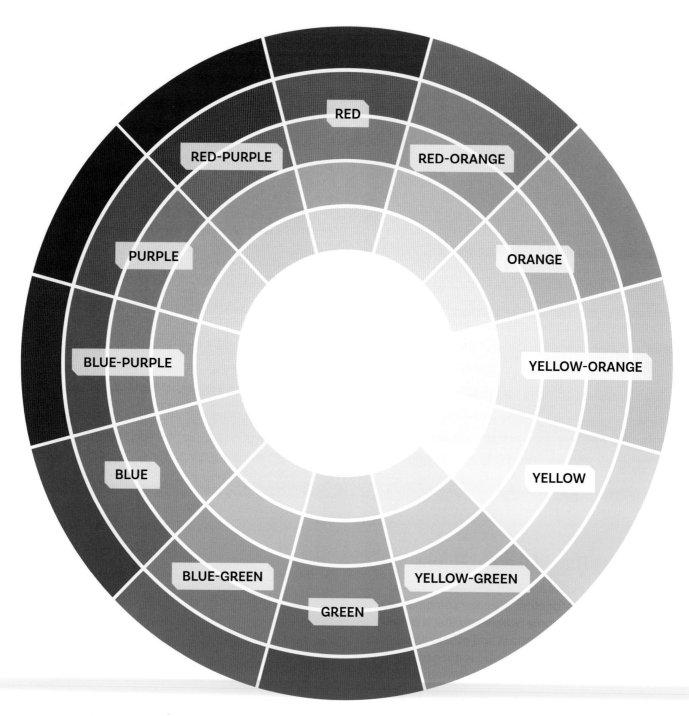

Use a color wheel to help guide your color choices. One easy trick for making a striking quilt is to mix and match colors that are across from each other on the wheel.

Finding Analogous Colors

Colors that are adjacent to each other on the color wheel are called analogous. Analogous colors help me transition from one color to another in the background of a quilt. I think of the colors as bleeding into one another. Looking at the color wheel helps me to remember that orange bleeds into red-orange, which bleeds into red. Or, moving in the opposite direction on the color wheel, orange bleeds into yellow-orange, which bleeds into yellow.

I chose orange for the background of *The Royal Ruminant* quilt on page 8 but did not have enough variety of pure orange fabrics to fill the background. Looking at the color wheel reminded me that I could bleed the color transition all the way from red to yellow on the background while still having the whole read as orange.

These autumn leaves look like a section of the color wheel, creating their own color transition as they move from red-purple all the way through green.

Finding Complementary Colors

Complementary colors are those that are directly across from each other on the color wheel. Complementary colors help each other shine when they are placed in the same composition. When they are placed next to each other, they give the quilt visual energy. Orange and blue are complementary to each other. Red-purple's complement is yellow-green.

When a color combination is not working and I feel stuck, I will pull out a color wheel and find the color that is complementary to the color of my main quilt focus. *The Royal Ruminant* has a blue fence in front of him because I wanted it to complement the orange background behind him. Orange and blue complementary colors came in handy again with the *Dashing Dog* project on page 95. The dog's orange-brown coat looked great against a blue background, as opposed to the green background I started with.

Using a direct complement may feel too cliché to you. If that's the case, try using a color that is adjacent to the complement. Use red-purple instead of purple when working with yellow. The colors will still look great together, but the combination is slightly less predictable.

Finding Variations

The color wheel shown on page 46 has five variations within each color. The middle ring is the base color, or the hue. The outer two rings are darker shades (the hue with black added), while the inner two rings are lighter tints (the hue with white added). This range shows how you can transition your colors from light to dark or include a range of values in one piece. The *Charming Chicken* project on page 89 has a variety of blue-greens behind her—some are lighter than others. Looking at the range of blue-greens between the lightest and darkest blue-green on the color wheel can be helpful in determining how to create a color wash in the background of the quilt.

The value range within one color also shows other options when looking at complementary colors. A light salmon (red-orange) might be the perfect choice to use in a blue-green quilt, where a true red-orange might be too vibrant.

Color Is Relative

When I am working with a specific fabric, I think about how it fits into a general rainbow classification—red, orange, yellow, green, blue, purple. I mentally file it into one of those simple buckets. Sometimes, colors fit into two buckets—a purple-tinted blue can fit in with the blues or the purples, which is why color wheels add in tertiary colors (the ones with two names like blue-purple). If you are not sure where a specific color

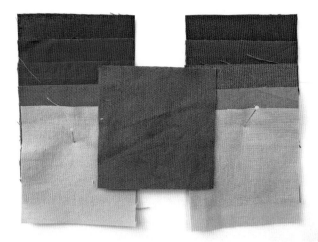

This blue-purple next to the purples on the right looks very blue. But it looks purple compared to the blues on the left. When sorting colors into groups, I would put this swatch into the blue side of the blue-purple spectrum.

This next statement is a gross simplification, but most neutrals, like browns and grays, are versions of the main hues of the color wheel. To determine which color family a specific brown or gray fabric belongs in, I place it next to other fabrics that I have already sorted into buckets. By testing it against other "known" colors, after a while,

you will be able to see if the fabric has warm (red, orange, or yellow) undertones or is based on a cooler color (blue, green, or purple). To keep things simple when I am sorting neutral fabrics, I do not try to fit them into the color wheel. I make two piles of browns, one warm and one cool, and do the same for grays.

Colors Don't Need to Match

When I worked at a quilt shop, helping customers pick out fabrics for their projects was my favorite part of the job. Sometimes a customer would come in with a focus fabric and want to exactly match other fabrics to it. While I understand the desire to mirror the color, it is hard to do when you are working with fabrics—each manufacturer, fabric line, and even dye lot is different from one another. What I learned at the shop is that the

> **TIP:** To see if a group of fabrics go together, don't look at them up close. Step back 10 feet and see how they look as a group. As with much of life, a little distance puts things in perspective.

Color Wheel Exercise #1— Make a Color Wheel Out of Solid Fabrics

Pull some solid fabrics out of your stash and sort the fabrics into color families—red, red-orange, orange, etc. Lay the piles in a circle around a color wheel (you can use the one on page 46 or print your own), mimicking the order of the printed wheel. When you do this, you may find that you have loads of one color and very few of another. I found that I had very few blues and lots of red-purples. Guess which color I love and which one I struggle to embrace? Because I just don't love blue and am not drawn to it, I do not buy very many blue fabrics. Notice which colors you are lacking in your color wheel and keep that in mind the next time you shop for fabric.

The Importance of Value

You thought this was a section about color, huh? Well, to paraphrase the old saying: color gets all the credit, but value does all the work. Have you ever seen a quilt that is dull and doesn't have much personality? Chances are that the colors in the quilt go together fine, but the quilt did not have enough value variety.

What Is Value?

Value is the relative lightness or darkness of a color. It is what is left if we strip out the color from the fabric and only see the whites, grays, and blacks within it. Having some contrast between dark and light is what gives quilts their sparkle. White next to dark gray creates tension and drama, while a medium gray next to another medium gray is ho-hum. We need both—the ho-hum helps the drama stand out. You know how blue skies look even more blue after a string of rainy days? That's how I think about value. Within each composition, there needs to be some cloudy and some sunny for the entire piece to shine. The lights and darks do not need to be in equal proportion to each other, but they each need to be present. Learning to see and incorporate value ranges is a skill that takes practice.

Color Wheel Exercise #2— Make a Color Wheel Sorted by Value

Using the same fabrics you organized in Exercise #1, sort each family from light to dark. Put the lightest of each color family close to the center of the wheel and the darkest on the outside ring. From each grouping, pick five fabrics that best make the transition from light to dark. (I cut 3" [7.6cm] squares out of these fabrics so that I could easily fold and pin them to my design wall while assessing my choices. This exercise is so satisfying when the swatches are organized like paint chip samples.)

Chances are that you will not have all the values/colors in your stash that are needed to complete a color wheel. That is ok. Do what you can and notice which colors and values you might be missing.

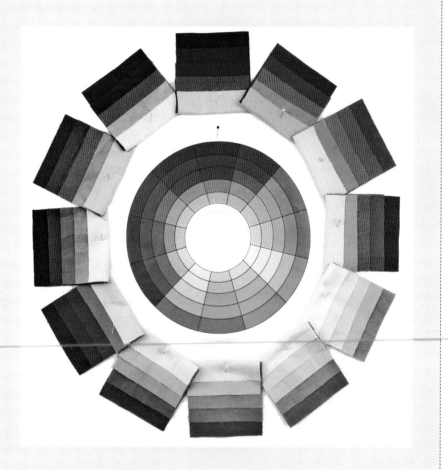

TIP: Spend some time looking for color combinations that you love. Grab a few art books from your local library, scroll online, or take notice of what grabs your eye in your everyday life.

Like Color, Value Is Relative

When we say that a color is light in value, it is only light in relation to other colors. Look at the green fabric value charts on the right. The one on the left is made with nine solid green fabrics organized in value order, the one on the right is made with printed fabrics. The strip running down the central column of each chart is the same fabric as the middle horizontal strip. Those strips are the middle-value in each group of fabrics. If I added two more darks to the bottom of the strips, the middle value would change. It would move down one place on the chart.

Notice how the middle value looks dark next to the light yellow-greens, but it looks light next to the dark greens at the bottom. You will also see that I have a wider value range of greens in my print stash than in my solid stash. The lights are lighter and the darks are darker in my printed fabrics, and the transition between each value is smoother. My solid chart has a big jump between light and dark because, apparently, I do not buy medium-value solid green fabrics!

These value charts easily demonstrate how a color's value relates to the values of the colors around it.

Color Wheel Exercise #3 — Make Your Own Value Charts

1. Find nine solid fabrics from one color family that range in value from light to dark.

2. Cut a 9" x 2½" (22.9 x 6.4cm) rectangle from each fabric and arrange them in order from light to dark. Once you are satisfied with the arrangement, sew the strips together along their 9" (22.9cm) sides, using a ¼" (6.4mm) seam allowance. Press the seams to one side.

3. Cut a 1½" x 18½" (3.8 x 47cm) strip from the middle value fabric and set it aside.

4. From the pieced strips, cut a 1" x 18½" (2.5 x 47cm) strip off the edge. Cut the remaining 8" (20.3cm) wide piece in half. You now have two 4" (10.2cm) strip sets.

5. Sew the reserved 1½" x 18½" (3.8 x 47cm) piece between the two 4" (10.2cm) strips of stripes, making sure the lightest stripes are at the top.

6. Turn the 1" x 18½" (2.5 x 47cm) strip 180 degrees and sew to one side of the value chart, with the darkest strip at the top.

7. Repeat steps 1–6 using printed fabrics to make a second chart.

Determining Value

- The first way I determine the value order of a pile of fabrics is to first sort them by eye. I squint and step back when I am doing this task. Sometimes I am literally too close to the fabrics to make an accurate determination. Some people can take off their glasses to help them see the change.

- Take a photo of the fabrics with your phone, then use the editing feature to change the photo to black and white. Once you can only see the black and white version, you will be able to determine if any fabrics seem out of place.

- Cut snippets from the fabrics you are considering and make a black and white photocopy that will show you the grayscale of the fabrics.

- Hold a red or green viewing filter close to your eyes. Looking through these translucent plastic rectangles helps neutralize the color and only shows you the value. One thing to be aware of though, the red viewing filter does not work on red fabrics and the green does not work on green material. Use the green on red fabrics and vice versa. One popular brand of color filter is the Ruby Ruler®, but you can also find them by searching for value finders, color evaluators, and color filters.

How Does Value "Do the Work"?

The Duchess of Dirt on page 14 has a purple snout and ears, even though in the reference photo those parts of her are pink and muddy. Since I did not have very many dark browns in my stash, I substituted another color of similar value. The viewer does not notice that the pig's snout is purple because the value is correct for the piece. The space under her chin is made up of greens. This works because the value is correct, not because her skin is actually green.

TIP: When planning fabrics for your next quilt, add in a few fabrics that are slightly lighter and darker than you would normally choose. Instead of using only cobalt blue, mix in a few pieces of navy and a bit of cerulean. Small variations in color and value add sparkle to quilts.

This photo shows the same green value charts from page 50 in black and white. If any of the values were out of place or out of order, it would be easy to spot without the distraction of color differences.

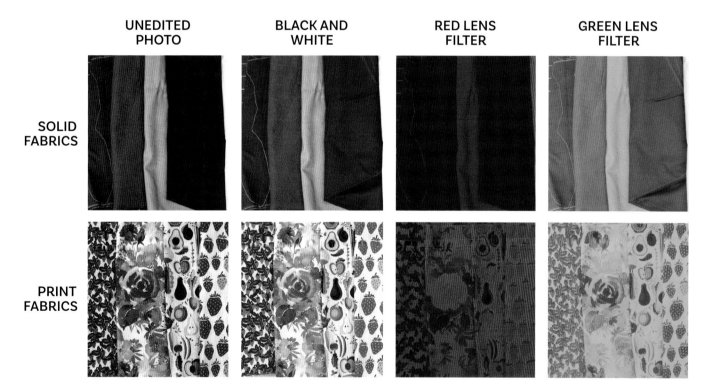

UNEDITED PHOTO	BLACK AND WHITE	RED LENS FILTER	GREEN LENS FILTER

SOLID FABRICS

PRINT FABRICS

The chart above shows two groups of fabrics and how they appear when using different value tools. The printed fabrics are organized by value order, while the blues are mixed up. Notice how the errant pink thread on the blue fabric on the left really stands out when filters are added. I did not see that thread until after I turned the photo to black and white and then it jumped right out at me. Using value tools can not only help you figure out fabric placement but can also help you see other problems in your composition that your eye may have missed earlier.

Using Value to Make Stitched Mosaic Images Stand Out

For an image to stand out, it needs to contrast with the background. Let's look at *The Hare Apparent* (page 14) below. For this quilt, I gave the hare a fuchsia (or red-purple) background. Since the hare has two wildly different values in her fur (a white chest versus black ears), I needed to pay attention to the placement of the background squares and how they would look next to her body. If I put the light pink squares that are currently in the upper right corner of the quilt next to her chest, her chest would blend right into the background. I placed the darkest fuchsias next to her chest and jowls to create a strong line separating the rabbit from the background. I know that a quilt is successful if I can change a photo of it to black and white and the image is still recognizable.

The importance of value and contrast is clear in *The Hare Apparent*, in which the main focus of the stitched mosaic quilt includes a stark contrast of blacks and whites.

The variation in values in this quilt's background is even easier to spot in black and white. The dark background at the bottom contrasts with the hare's white chest, and the lighter squares at the top contrast with her black ears.

Low-Volume Fabrics

Recently in the quilting world, there has been a trend toward using what are called "low-volume" fabrics. These are printed fabrics that are light in value and have minimal contrast between them. The prints tend to be subtle and "quiet." The body in *The Hare Apparent* above is one example of how low-volume prints can be used. The prints read as solid from a distance but give a bit of visual texture with their patterns. When making this quilt, at one point, I realized that I did not have enough value change distinguishing her chin and neck. To remedy that problem, I used some slightly darker low-volume prints under the rabbit's mouth and on her chin to create a value change between that and her neck. Keep in mind that even though low-volume fabrics are generally light in color, there is still a spectrum of values within them.

Solids versus Prints

Solid fabrics are pure, joyful bursts of color, but prints really have my heart. Prints give a fabric, and consequently a finished quilt, layers of visual texture that cannot be achieved with only solids. I find that it is easier to blend printed fabrics from one color or value with another because there are a variety of shapes and colors within each piece. When using solids, there is often an abrupt transition from one fabric to another. It is easier for me to finesse a transition between prints.

While I find prints easier to use, sorting them into color families is less clear-cut than sorting solids. I decide which pile to put a fabric into based on the "general impression" that fabric gives me. This is where stepping back and getting some distance from what I am looking at is crucial. I do not want to get hung up on any details in the print.

For some prints, it's easy to determine in which color family to place them. For others, especially those with large prints, it can be harder. Don't spend too much time thinking about sorting your fabrics with large patterns. Instead, make a quick decision. You may change your mind later, and that's okay. This is a fluid process.

Color Wheel Exercise #4—Make a Color Wheel with Prints

Follow the steps in Exercise #1, using printed fabrics rather than solids.

Since we are working with 2½" (5.1cm) squares when making stitched mosaics, you can always cut a square out of a large print and see which family that particular square belongs to. It may fall into a different color family than a square cut from a different part of the fabric.

While large prints can be challenging to use, they can also act as transitional fabrics between colors. The group of blue fabrics in the top photo below does not

This photo shows some of the difficulty of blending fabrics with large prints into a composition. The jump from the navy fabric on the left and the floral fabric next to it is very sharp.

One small change (adding in the larger floral print second from the left) can make a huge difference in how well the fabrics transition one to another.

Adding in a slightly larger large floral print, as shown in the bottom photo, however, can link the pieces together. Not only do the colors work well, but the transition also feels more natural. Several of these fabrics were used in the background of the *Dashing Dog* project on page 96.

> **TIP:** There are no rules as to what fabrics to use in your piece. Mix up your batiks, prints, and solids. Use the wrong side of the fabrics. Sometimes flipping the square over and using the backside will give you just the color or value you've been looking for. Throw in a square of the feed sack you've been saving. I've been known to buy shirts at discount stores just to cut them up into 2½" (6.4cm) squares. I do try to stick to 100% cotton fabric, but the most important feature is "does the fabric have the right color and pattern to help create the image I'm working on?" If yes, I'll use it!

Why Use So Many Fabrics in One Quilt?

I find that it is easier to transition colors and values through eighty different fabrics than it is to move through eight. The fewer fabrics you use in a piece, the more important it is that each fabric is "perfect" for the composition. If one fabric is not exactly right, it will throw off the whole design. When there are eighty different fabrics, the few clunkers you might have to include will blend in with the rest. Because I use many small pieces in my quilts, I'm always scavenging through my friends' scrap bins so that I can supplement my own scraps with colors and textures I would not usually buy. When I purchase fabric, I buy ¼ yd. or ⅓ yd. (22.9 or 30.5cm) at a time. I would rather have eight different, but similar, greens than 2 yds. (1.8m) of the same green. Using a larger variety of fabrics helps inspire creativity and reduces waste!

Color Wheel Exercise #5—Make a Color Wheel with Prints Sorted by Value

Follow the steps used in Exercise #2, using the printed fabrics you organized in Exercise #4. While the solids will look like paint chips, the prints look more like wallpaper samples. Notice in the photo on the left how the transitions are smoother than in the solids example—the transitions are more organic and less regular.

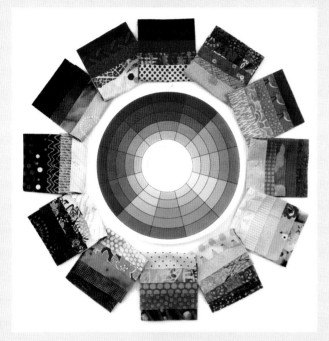 

The color wheel on the right includes both solids and prints. The inner ring is light solids, which transition into the dark solids. Then the dark prints move toward the lights on the outside. I really love how I can start with a pile of unorganized fabrics, and just by sorting them by color and then by value, the chaos is controlled into something quite beautiful.

Auditioning Fabric and Color Placement

Before I start sewing a stitched mosaic piece, I cut out many different 2½" (6.4cm) squares of fabrics that fit my rule for the piece or are colors or patterns that I think will work for the coloring of the main subject. I then sort those squares into rough piles based on their color and value, so I can see what I have and what I need more of. For example, when beginning the *Charming Chicken* project on page 89, I ended up with two sets of squares: blue-greens for the background and blacks and whites for her feathers.

This range of blue-green squares is what I came up with when organizing fabrics for the background of the Charming Chicken project.

In contrast, I organized blacks, whites, and dark blues by value so the chicken's feathers would pop against the blue-green background.

This is just a place to start. Once I start placing the squares next to each other, I discard some and add others depending on how they all work together. Once I have a stack of fabrics to work with, I pin them directly on top of the photo, which I've attached to a piece of foam core. I always start by laying out the background, mostly because that is the easiest part for me to arrange. It also helps define the main figure by blocking out any extraneous background clutter I don't want in the final quilt.

Here you can see how I've folded, overlapped, and adjusted my squares to give a good idea of what the background will look like using the blue-green fabrics (and what the chicken will look like against that background).

This photo shows this "shaggy" part of *The Hare Apparent* in process, testing the combination of background pink fabrics against the whites and blacks of the hare.

When pinning fabric squares to the foam core, the squares will not fit together perfectly since they are ½" (1.3cm) bigger than the drawn squares. Overlap and fold the fabric as necessary to help you visualize. Remember, this is the "shaggy" part of the process. Even though it feels messy, it will clean up nicely when you start sewing your pieces and squares together.

If the squares on the photograph have more than one color in them, fold the fabrics to approximate the finished shape and pin them to the board. This will give you a sense of the proportion of color within the block. It will also help you start to think about how to layer the elements of the block. Which fabric should be the base? Which one should you layer on top next? It's only after I

Here is a good example of how folding and pinning the individual fabric squares and pinning them to the photo on the foam core can help you envision how the final block should look and how to best construct it.

Let the Fabric Do the Work

Printed fabrics can do much of the visual heavy lifting when making a stitched mosaic quilt. The printed patterns add texture and dimension. Let's stay with the fabrics for the *Charming Chicken* for the next example. We can see in the original photo on page 57 that her feathers transition from white to black as they move from her head to her tail, and some of her feathers are striped. It would be an immense amount of work to replicate every stripe and detail with appliqué. Instead, I used black and white fabrics, many of which have stripes in them, to create the visual cue of striped feathers. While her tail feathers are a glossy black in real life, I used mostly black and dark blue fabrics for those.

The original inspiration photo for the *Charming Chicken* project includes an abundance of textural detail within the feathers.

The first thing I did when deciding on which fabrics to use for her full range of feathers was to cut a stack of 2½" (6.4cm) squares of solid white fabrics, solid black or dark fabrics, and mixed black-and-white fabrics. I then sorted them roughly by color and by value. Once the squares were sorted into families, I had a good idea of where to put them on the chicken. The lightest whites went on her head while the darkest darks ended up on

The final quilt makes use of patterns within the fabric blocks to give the impression of the color shift and texture of the feathers.

Occasionally you will find a print that integrates seamlessly into your composition. The Kaffe Fassett for Rowan Westminster Fibers Cabbage and Rose printed fabric shown in the photo below is perfect for chicken combs and wattles. When the print is cut into small pieces, the fabric replicates the fleshy bits and undulations of those body parts perfectly. Certain low-volume prints work very well to mimic the pattern and texture of fur and certain fabrics that read overall as one color may actually work as a completely different color when you focus in on a small part of the print. Poke through your stash with an eye toward the possibilities of what your fabric **COULD** be.

This cabbage rose fabric is perfect for conveying the red color and texture of chicken combs, wattles, and lobes.

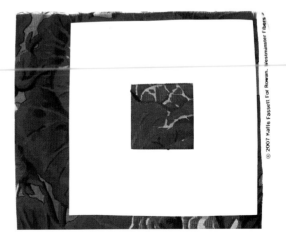

TIP: To audition a fabric and see how it will look when cut into small pieces, use a 2" (5.1cm) square hole cut in a larger piece of cardstock as a window to frame a smaller piece of the fabric.

CHAPTER 3:
Basic Construction Techniques—Blue Daisy

 Blue Daisy—Finished quilt
11" x 11" (27.9 x 27.9cm)

This daisy project walks you step-by-step through the skills you need to make a stitched mosaic project from your own photo. Use these same techniques to play with color and construction in the simpler practice project included at the end of this chapter (see page 70).

FABRIC AND PAPER REQUIREMENTS

- 2½" (6.4cm) squares of assorted fabrics, approximately forty-four each of blues and whites, and four yellows
- 16" x 16" (40.6 x 40.6cm) batting
- 16" x 16" (40.6 x 40.6cm) backing fabric
- Two 2¼" (5.7cm) WOF (width-of-fabric) strips for binding
- Forty 2" (5.1cm) squares of freezer paper
- One copy of the original daisy photo on page 122, enlarged by 165% so that the photo prints at 12" x 12" (30.5 x 30.5cm) and prepared as shown on page 41 of Chapter 1

To help you focus on the technique, pick two main colors to work with—one for the flower, another for the background—then choose an assortment of fabrics that blend well together within each color family. I used a medley of medium blues for the petals and whites for the background. Because there is a stark value contrast between the white and blue, the daisy jumps forward. If you decide to put your flower on a green, leafy background, make sure that either the daisy or the background is lighter in value than the other element. Without that contrast, the daisy will blend

Work One Square at a Time

Compare the original unmarked image on the left with the prepared printout on the right.

The stitched mosaic method asks you to look at, and replicate in fabric, only one square of the photo at a time. If you need help focusing on a specific square, cut a 2" (5.1cm) hole out of a larger piece of cardstock and place the opening over the working square (see the photo below). This is especially helpful since I only want you to make what your eyes see, not what your brain knows. You may know that there are two petals in a square. If your eye can't distinguish them, forget that you know that information. When you get to a square

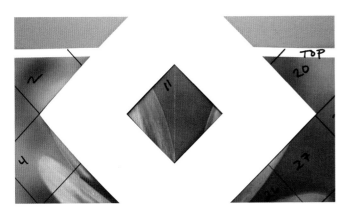

Cutting a 2" (5.1cm) square hole in a larger piece of cardstock makes a low-tech tool that will help you focus only on the square you want to work on.

Think in Layers

Most blocks are constructed in layers. There is a base layer, with other fabrics appliquéd on top of it. Often the base layer is the color that you will see the most of, while the smaller pieces appliquéd on top are the other color (or multiple other colors if your design is more complicated). When getting started, I suggest beginning with a square that has only one or two elements in it. Once you pick which square to start with, decide the order in which to layer the fabrics.

Some blocks do not need any appliqué, such as squares #1 and #2 in the upper left corner. For those squares, you can pick two of the white background fabric squares, sew them together with a

You may be wondering why the fabric is cut at 2½" (6.4cm) while the freezer paper is cut at 2" (5.1cm). It's simple—the fabric squares include seam allowances, but the freezer paper pieces will become your templates, so they do not include seam allowances.

Make the Templates

Let's start with square #11. It is a two-layer square with a white background fabric base and blue flower petal fabric appliquéd on top.

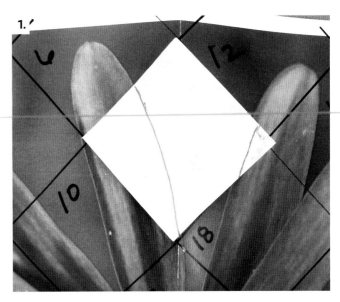

1. Place a 2" (5.1cm) square of freezer paper shiny side up on top of the square you are replicating and use a light-colored ultra fine point marker to trace the shapes in the

2.

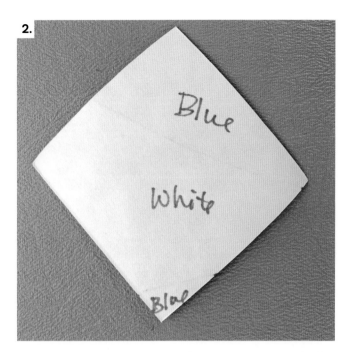

2. On the dull paper side of the freezer paper, note which color belongs to each shape. If you need to make any other notes to yourself, do it on the paper side of the freezer paper. It's important to put any notes on the paper side since that is the side that you will be able to see while you prepare the appliqué pieces.

TIP: Avoid getting the freezer paper wet if you can help it. Occasionally the marker lines will bleed when they get wet, but I don't worry about it, as it is rarely seen in the final product.

3.

3. Cut the freezer paper square apart along the

4.

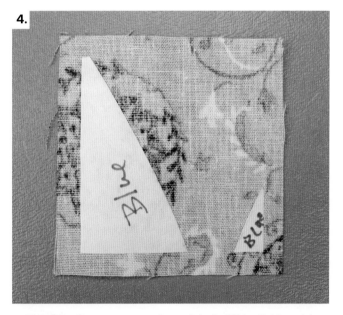

4. Place the freezer paper pieces labeled "blue" shiny side down on the back of a piece of blue fabric. Leave at least a ¼" (6.4mm) of extra fabric around the outside of each freezer paper template. Iron in place.

5.

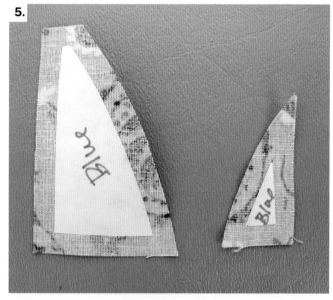

5. Cut around the freezer paper templates, leaving a ¼" (6.4mm) seam allowance.

TIP: If it's difficult to see through the freezer paper to trace the shapes, use a light box or tape the photo to a sunny window while you draw your lines.

Prepared-Edge Appliqué

Seam allowances that fall within the 2" (5.1cm) block need to be turned under. These seams will be appliquéd down. Seam allowances that fall along the perimeter of the block should not be turned under. Those edges will be hidden once the block is joined to its neighboring blocks. It is important that the perimeter edges have an accurate ¼" (6.4mm) seam allowance so that the finished blocks fit together well when you piece them together.

Two Layers

The easiest blocks to make using prepared-edge appliqué consist of two layers: your base fabric and the top piece being appliquéd to the base fabric.

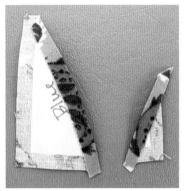

1. Pour a small amount of your favorite starch or starch alternative into a shallow bowl. Use a small paintbrush to paint a little of the liquid on the seam allowances you need to turn under. In square #11, the curved edges of the

2. Fold the starched seam allowances over to the paper side of the freezer paper and set them with a dry iron. Use your finger or a

3. Remove the freezer paper from the fabric and dab a glue stick on the turned edges. Then place the blue pieces glue side down in the appropriate locations on the white background square. Touch them with a hot iron to secure them in place. If

4. Machine appliqué the blue pieces down. See Machine Appliqué Basics on pages 62–65.

5. Cut the excess background fabric from behind the appliqué, leaving a ¼" (6.4mm) seam allowance inside the stitching line. This removes extra bulk from the quilt top.

TIP: To make sure my ironing mat stays clean, I keep a small scrap of cotton batting on top of it. While I paint the seam allowances around the freezer paper templates, I keep them on the batting to absorb any extra liquid.

Machine Appliqué Basics

Once you've finished turning under your edges and adhering your appliqué pieces together, all your turned-under edges need to be anchored with stitching. I do not put a stabilizer behind the blocks since they have plenty of body from starch and glue. I usually use a blanket stitch to sew my appliqué down. It is a sturdy stitch and is forgiving on curves. If your machine doesn't have a blanket stitch, use a zigzag stitch or something similar. A straight stitch will work, as well. Test which stitch works best for you on scraps of fabric before starting on your project.

I almost always want my appliqué stitches to be hidden, but for these example photos, I used black thread so you can see all the details. In real life, I don't want any imperfections to be visible, which is why I use (and love) monofilament thread.

BLANKET STITCH

1. Adjust the size of the stitch on the machine to approximately a 1.7mm width and 2mm length. If applicable, set your machine to stop with the needle down.

2. Sew a few stitches onto a piece of scrap fabric or batting. This scrap is sometimes called a spider. With the threads still attached, pull the spider back behind the foot. The spider keeps the threads taut and keeps them from getting tangled in the bobbin area or making nests on the back of your sewing. Spiders are especially important if you are using monofilament thread since the thread is hard to see and keep track of. Make sure that both the top and bobbin threads are underneath the foot.

3. Start stitching your appliqué piece onto the base. The needle should travel in the ditch on the base layer and then take little bites into the appliqué piece. The bite stitches should be perpendicular to the traveling stitches. In this case, the needle travels in the red fabric right next to the blue fabric and takes bites into the blue.

4. To change directions, or to adjust on a curve, stop with the needle down in the "ditch" at the end of a base fabric stitch, rather than after a "bite" into the appliqué piece, then raise the presser foot slightly and rotate the fabric as needed. For curves, you may need only a slight adjustment. It's important to stop in the ditch so that the bite stitches do not get distorted. Stop and adjust as many times as needed.

5. After stitching to the end of the seam, lift the presser foot and pull the block back behind the foot a few inches, with the threads still attached. Clip off the threads from the block (the block should still be attached to the spider, however). Bring the spider around to the front and sew a few stitches onto it so that it is ready to go for the next piece.

6. Free the block from the spider by clipping the threads between them, then cut out the extra fabric from behind the block. Your appliqué block is ready to be joined into your quilt.

For blocks that need to be appliquéd starting or ending in the middle of the block, you can still follow the instructions above. The only difference is that if you start or end a stitch line in the middle of a block, you need to backstitch so the stitches do not unravel. Again, always travel in the ditch and bite into the piece that needs to be secured.

Notice the thicker stitches between the polka-dotted fabric pieces at the center of this block. Those stitches have been backstitched.

When stitching an outer or inner point, make sure to put the needle down in the ditch side and pivot the fabric as needed. This will keep the bite stitches perpendicular to the seam line. If you need to tuck under a seam allowance, use a stiletto to help guide the seam where you want it. Stilettos can also help keep wiggly appliqué pieces in place as you stitch them down.

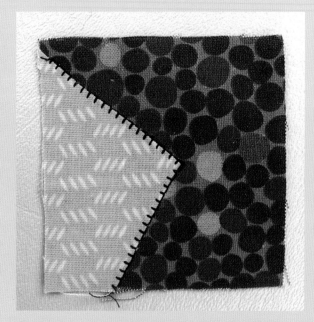 

Whether you are sewing an outer point (left) or an inner point (right), be certain to stop at the end of a ditch-side stitch, with your needle down in the base fabric, before turning your fabric.

A stiletto is very useful to keep fabric in place while you sew or for tucking extra seam allowance fabric under.

ZIGZAG STITCH

When using a zigzag stitch to anchor your appliqué, you will probably need to adjust the zigzag width and length from the machine's factory settings. I set mine to a 2.5mm width and 1mm length. Have the right position of the needle hit in the ditch of the base fabric and the left position go into the appliqué piece. When adjusting the fabric to accommodate curves or direction changes, stop with the needle down in the base layer, lift the presser foot, and adjust the block as necessary.

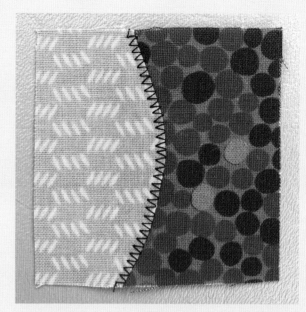

When you use a zigzag stitch, be sure that every right-hand stitch is going into the base fabric and every left-hand stitch is going into the top appliqué fabric piece.

STRAIGHT STITCH

For straight-line appliqué, stitch on top of the appliqué piece about 1⁄16" (1.6mm) inside the turned-under edge. Go slowly around curves so that the line is very smooth. A short stitch length (approximately 1.8–2mm) will help keep the stitching line smooth as you sew around curves. If you need to stop and adjust as you sew, stop with the needle down.

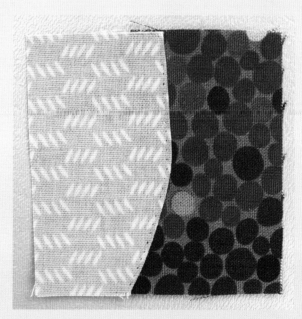

These two photos show similar blocks appliquéd with a straight stitch. Here you can clearly see the difference monofilament thread makes.

Three or More Layers

In this daisy, the more complicated blocks are in the center of the flower. These blocks have three colors and multiple layers to contend with. Let's look at square #24.

Determine in which order to layer the fabrics. In block #24, I use white as the base layer again, even though very little of it shows up in the finished block. The base gives the block a structural foundation on which to attach the appliqué. Blue is the second layer, and yellow is the third and final layer. I chose this order because the tips of the petals can be tucked under the yellow of the flower's center, saving the step of needing to turn under those edges.

Remember that you can always simplify to create a more striking quilt. Notice that I only approximated the general shape of the yellow stamen in my template. Replicating every tiny filament on such a small scale would be overwhelming. Rather than adding the detail now, texture can be added after the quilt top is pieced together. I'm partial to adding texture with quilting thread, but beads, embroidery, and other embellishments are also great ways to fill in tiny details.

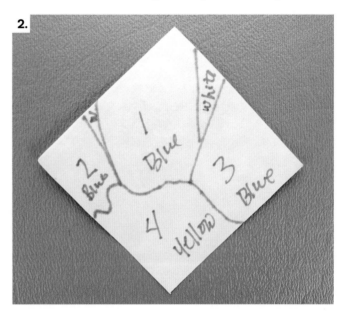

2. Label the color of each shape and the order in which they'll be placed on the paper side of the freezer paper. Notice that petal #3 will overlap petal #1 slightly.

1. Place a 2" (5.1cm) piece of freezer paper shiny side up on top of the square you are replicating and use a light-colored ultra fine point marker to trace the shapes onto the freezer paper.

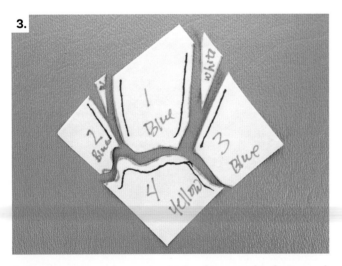

3. On the paper side, mark which edges need to be turned under. For complicated blocks, I draw a line (in this case red) along the edges that will need to be turned under so

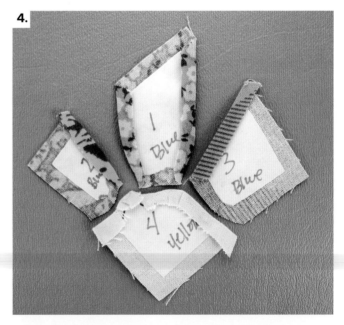

4. Iron the freezer paper templates shiny side down to the back of the fabrics, then cut them out, leaving a ¼" (6.4mm) seam allowance. Turn the appropriate edges under, following steps 1 and 2 on page 61.

5.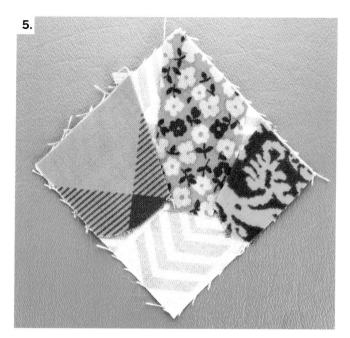

6.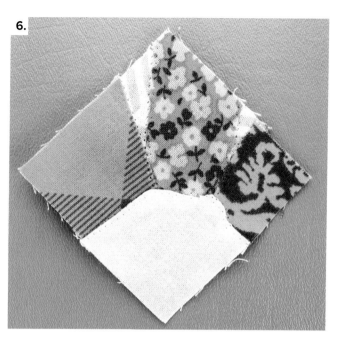

5. Remove the freezer paper from the blue fabric and dab a glue stick on the turned edges. Then place the blue pieces glue side down in the appropriate locations on the white background square. Touch them with a hot iron to secure them in place. Repeat for the yellow piece

6. Machine appliqué all the pieces down. See Machine Appliqué Basics on pages 62–65.

7.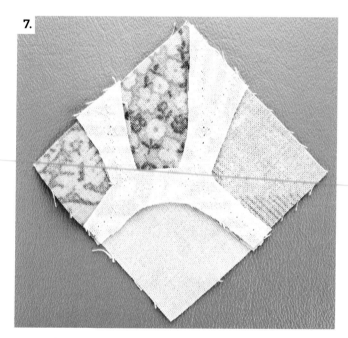

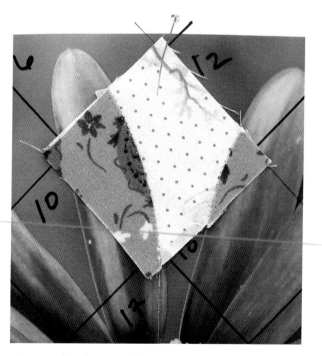

7. Cut the excess background fabric from behind the appliqué, leaving a ¼" (6.4mm) seam allowance inside the

TIP: I pin the photo and the completed blocks to a piece of foam core. This helps me keep the blocks organized and lets me watch the quilt develop as I work. There is something very satisfying about covering up the photo with fabric piece by piece. The foam core is also light enough that I can pin it to my design wall and work on the project vertically, freeing up valuable table space.

Finishing the Stitched Mosaic Quilt

Repeat the prepared-edge appliqué process as needed for all the numbered squares in the photo. If you pin the completed squares to the photo as you work, you'll easily know when they're all ready to be combined.

1. Sew the blocks together in rows with ¼" (6.4mm) seams, using cotton thread.

Experiment by mixing up the colors. In this example, I switched the blue and white fabrics to create a white daisy. Maybe you want a pink or an orange daisy? Have fun trying out the colors that inspire you and make you happy.

TIP: I press my seams to the side, alternating direction with each row. Odd rows (the first row, third row, fifth row, etc.) are all pressed to the left, while even rows (the second row, fourth row, sixth row, etc.) are all pressed to the right. This allows my seams to nest together nicely when the rows are sewn together. As long as I know what row number I'm on, I know which direction to press the seams when I get to my ironing board.

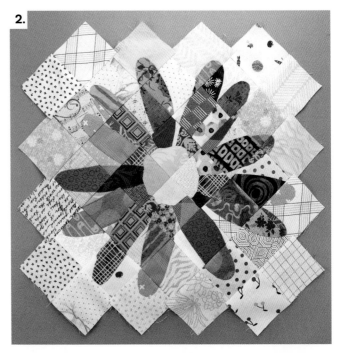

2. When all the rows are assembled, sew them together. Keep the zigzag edges of the quilt top intact until after it is quilted. Trimming the squares corner-to-corner creates bias edges, which are stretchy. Quilting stabilizes the quilt and helps keep everything aligned until you are ready to square up the quilt in preparation for binding.

3. Layer with batting and backing and quilt as desired, then bind and add a hanging sleeve. See Chapter 7 for more details on finishing your pieces.

Your first of many stitched mosaic masterpieces is complete!

Key Points to Consider

- Only think about one 2" (5.1cm) square at a time. You do not need to tackle the whole quilt at once.

- Think in layers. When thinking about each block's construction, decide on the base layer fabric first, then pick the fabrics to put on top of it. The base layer is often the fabric that makes up the biggest percentage of the block.

- Simplify. There is a temptation to add in every detail. Consider what a viewer will see if they are standing ten feet away from the finished piece and focus on those elements.

- Trust what you see, not what you think you should see.

- Value is more important than color. If you do not have the exact color needed, find a color that is similar and has an equal lightness or darkness as your desired color. The final product will often be made more interesting by color variations.

- Add as many different fabrics as you can. That is what gives the quilt visual density.

- When you sew the blocks together, the composition lines from one square to the next probably will not match at the seam. No need to worry! The viewer's eye will complete the line and visually smooth it out.

- Take a break when needed. The quilt will wait for you.

You may find that when your blocks are sewn together, the appliquéd shapes do not line up exactly from block to block. That is okay and part of the charm of this process. The seam lines act as a small visual break between the blocks, much like the grout does in tile mosaics. Our eyes smooth the transition between blocks when we look at the finished product. Once your blocks are sewn together, step back and look at the flower from several feet away. You will be amazed at how it comes together.

Bonus Practice Project

Rhubarb Leaf

The pink and green of rhubarb is one of my favorite color combinations. I'm always excited when the rhubarb comes up in the spring because it means there is rhubarb crisp in my future. This young rhubarb leaf is the perfect beginner project. All you need are three shades of green fabrics and three shades of pink fabrics. The pattern can be photocopied on standard paper on your home printer, so there's no need for a special trip to the print shop! Once you've made this practice project, try making it

Rhubarb Leaf—Finished quilt 8½" x 11" (21.6 x 27.9cm)

FABRIC AND PAPER REQUIREMENTS

- 2½" (6.4cm) squares of assorted fabrics, approximately:
  - 29 light pink squares (for background)
  - 1 light pink square (for stem)
  - 2 medium pink squares (for stem)
  - 3 light green squares (for leaf highlights)
  - 10 medium green squares (for leaf)
  - 9 dark green squares (for leaf)
- 12" x 14" (30.5 x 35.6cm) batting
- 12" x 14" (30.5 x 35.6cm) backing fabric
- One and one half 2¼" (5.7cm) WOF (width-of-fabric) strips for binding
- Thirteen 2" (5.1cm) squares of freezer paper
- A copy of the rhubarb leaf photo on page 124 printed at 8½" x 11" (21.6 x 27.9cm).

Choosing Fabrics

My leaf has a large value contrast within it. If you would like your leaf to be more subtle, choose greens that are closer together in value (a little less dark and a little less light). I chose to use a pale pink in the background behind my leaf because I wanted the leaf to pop out. This works not just because it's a dark leaf on a light background, but because the pink and green are complementary colors. Also, rather than trying to create the veining in the leaf with fabric, I quilted veins in using a gold thread. This simplifies the construction process while adding some striking detail.

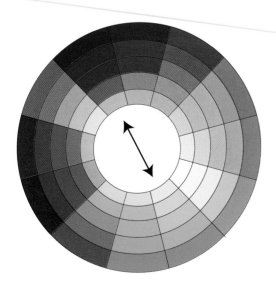

This color wheel shows why the light pink background works so well to highlight the green rhubarb leaf—working with complementary colors is always a good choice.

This photo of a young rhubarb leaf is clean and simple, the perfect inspiration for an easier, but still elegant and impressive, art quilt.

Construction

1. Prepare the photo as described in Chapter 1. If there are any shapes in the photo that need clarification, use your black marker to define the edges, especially the light and dark areas inside the leaf.

2. Pin the background fabric squares to the grid of the photo (remember to pin the photo on foam core).

3. Once you are happy with the arrangement, do the same with the leaf and stem squares.

4. Prepare the blocks and machine appliqué any squares that need to be stitched. For more information on basic construction review the rest of Chapter 3.

5. Sew the squares together in diagonal rows. Then sew the rows together.

6. Layer the top on the batting and backing.

7. Quilt as desired. See suggestions below and Chapter 6 for more details.

8. Square up and trim all the layers. My quilt is trimmed to about 8½" x 11" (21.6 x 27.9cm).

9. Bind and label the quilt. See Chapter 6 for more details.

Tip for Tricky Elements

Though simpler than the other projects in this book, there are still some details that might be trickier or require special techniques or guidance. Here is one tip to make things easier.

Turning Edges Under—Block #22

Block #22 is not hard to make, but it does take a little planning to decide which raw edges will be tucked under the turned edges of the adjacent pieces. I turned under all the inner edges of the largest dark green piece and tucked the medium green pieces underneath it. The smallest dark green piece is tucked under the turned edge of the medium green piece it sits next to. Remember that you do not need to turn under any edges that fall on the perimeter of the 2½" (6.4cm) square, as they will be hidden in the seam allowances when the blocks are sewn together.

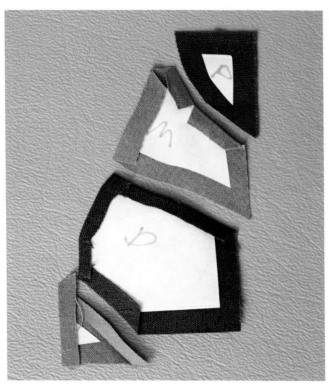

Here you can see the backs of the fabric pieces used to create the part of the leaf in Block #22. Any edges that haven't been turned under will be left raw and tucked beneath the edges of the adjacent pieces.

Finished Block #22 shows how the turned edges overlap the raw edges. The largest dark green piece, for example, had all three inside edges turned under, so it slightly overlaps the adjacent pieces.

Quilting Suggestions

Other than the gold stitching used to create the veins in the leaf, I used simple quilting on the background to further emphasize the rhubarb leaf.

CHAPTER 4:
Troubleshooting Tips and Tricks

Now that you have the basic stitched mosaic technique mastered and are ready to tackle quilts inspired by more complicated photos, you may come across more complex shapes. In this chapter, I will show you some of the common challenges you might face and how I approach them. Keep in mind that each individual block has its own quirks,

A Tip for Templates—Where Is the Line?

There will be times when you will not be able to see through the freezer paper and won't know where to draw the template line. I handle this by marking the beginning and ending of the line at the edges of the freezer paper. These points are easy to find because the line often runs into adjacent squares. Once the starting and ending points are marked, I connect the two points by estimating the general shape of the line.

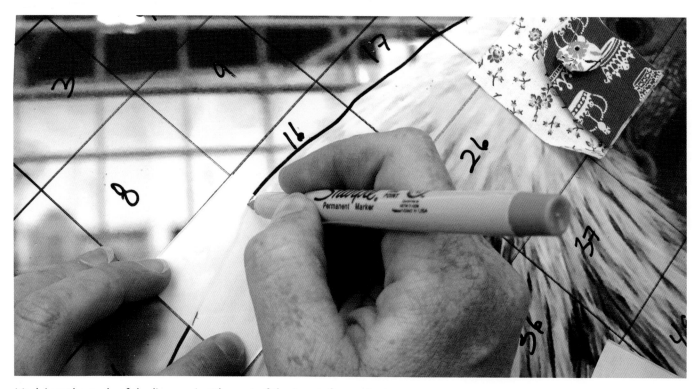

Mark just the ends of the lines, using the rest of the image for context.

Connect the two ends you drew, estimating the shape of the line in between. The line doesn't need to be exact; it just needs to work with the squares surrounding it.

Appliqué Placement—Where Does This Piece Go Again?

One thing that regularly happens is that I forget where the appliqué shapes belong on the background square. The first thing to do is to look back at the reference photo. In a lot of ways, this process is like simultaneously designing and assembling a jigsaw puzzle. If you suspect that a square might be challenging, take a photo of the freezer paper square that has the template lines drawn on it before you cut it apart.

Right Angles

The best clue as to where to place shapes is to look at the perimeter of the appliqué piece. If it has a 90-degree corner, that corner will likely match with one of the corners on the base layer. If the appliqué piece has only one right-angle corner, place the prepared shape on the base, stacking the corners on top of each other. If the background fabric is directional (such as stripes going in a specific direction), make sure that the pieces are oriented correctly before stitching them together.

Look for and match 90-degree corners on your appliqué pieces if you're having trouble remembering the proper arrangement. Corners are useful landmarks for lining up the pieces of a block.

Appliqué pieces that have two or more outside corner edges are the easiest to place. Put the appliqué piece on top of the base square, making sure that the two corners of the top appliqué piece are lined up with two of the corners on the base square. Again, be aware of any

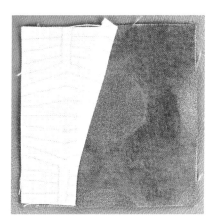

Pieces with multiple corners are easy to place. You can often just line them up with one side of your base fabric.

Floating Pieces

Sometimes you will find an appliqué piece that is floating on its own without any reference points. The shape extends to the perimeter of a block, but it does not cover a corner. An easy way to determine placement is to use the freezer paper square as a guide.

1. Prepare the appliqué shapes as usual but keep the extra "waste" piece of paper left over after cutting out the template. This "waste" is the negative space around the shape and can be used as a mask.

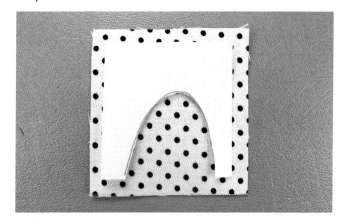

2. Place the mask shiny side up on the base fabric, leaving ¼" (6.4mm) seam allowances along all the edges.

3. Place the prepared appliqué shape in the hole. If it seems to be backwards or doesn't fit in the hole easily, double-check that the shiny side of the mask is facing the correct direction. Since the template would correctly be arranged shiny side up (being stuck to the back side of the appliqué piece), the shiny sides of both pieces of freezer paper need to be facing this same direction for the puzzle to fit together correctly.

Turning Curved Edges

Rounded pieces and curves are always easier to deal with than pointy pieces or blunt ends. Outer (convex) and inner (concave) curves are treated differently. Seam allowances that wrap around a gentle outer curve of a template are easy to manipulate and bend around the freezer paper. You just need to be careful that the fabric wraps around smoothly and doesn't have any jagged points along the edge. (See Fixing Jagged Edges on page 77.)

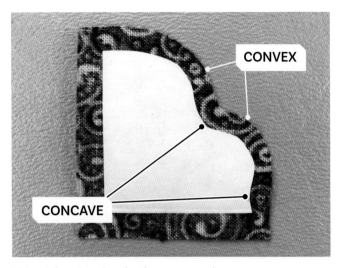

This tricky piece has both convex and concave curves.

Using small, sharp scissors will help you make precise cuts that will allow you to fold the fabric smoothly.

Inner curves require clipping the seam allowance inside the curve. When not clipped, the fabric remains taut and will not turn easily around the freezer paper template. Clipping allows the fabric to bend around the curve. This is a common technique used in garment making for setting in sleeves and making necklines. With small, sharp scissors, snip the seam allowance from the outer edge of the fabric right up to the freezer paper in the concave areas. The number of snips needed depends on the length and depth of the curve but placing a cut every ¼" (6.4mm) is a good rule of thumb. Since all these pieces are machine appliquéd along the folded edge, there's no need to worry about fraying. The machine stitches will hold everything neatly in place.

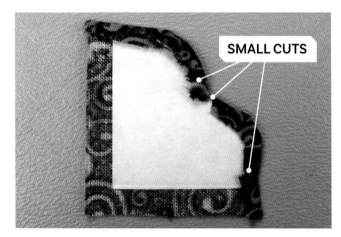

Notice that the fabric is clipped in two places on the deeper inner curve and only once in the shallow curve at the bottom right.

When I work on a stitched mosaic piece, I tend to make one block at a time, and I hold onto all the paper pieces in a block until after the whole block is made. Those tiny pieces of paper have a lot of information on them. Not only do they include the template shapes, but they also have any notes that I may have made when drawing. After several times spent fishing through the trash can looking for little pieces that I tossed before finishing the block, I became more religious about keeping this system.

On the flip side, once I am finished with a block, I throw out all the paper and fabric detritus. That way I know when I start the next block, I won't accidentally mix any block pieces together. I keep a small bin on my ironing board (shown in the photo on the left) within easy reach just for paper and fabric scraps. Everything I may need for preparing appliqué pieces is handy.

Fixing Jagged Edges

When turning seam allowances to the uncoated paper side of the freezer paper, even with careful attention to detail and the best of intentions, sometimes little points and jagged edges happen. To smooth out the edges, dip a paintbrush in your favorite starch or starch alternative and dab it gently on the problem spot. Pull the fabric around to the paper side so that it hugs the template and iron until it's dry. If there are a few places that need correction, dab each spot individually. Be cautious not to use too much liquid, as you do not want soggy paper.

After initially turning over the edges, this piece still had some jagged points sticking out from the curves.

Use a brush to gently dab each jagged point, then pull it to the back and iron it until it's dry.

The finished piece with the curved edges turned over and the jagged points corrected. It's ready to be appliquéd to the base fabric.

TIP: When freezer paper templates get soggy from too much starch, they cannot hold their shape. One way to remedy that problem is to iron them again until they are dry and then start over with painting the seam allowances. If the templates are wet and distorted and you are frustrated, throw them away and re-trace your lines onto another piece of freezer paper. Or put everything aside and come back tomorrow after you have eaten and had some sleep. Sometimes starting over or taking a break is the easiest way to accomplish the task. It always makes things better in my studio!

Inner or Outer Curve—Which Piece Should Be the Base Layer?

On Block #6 of the *Blue Daisy* in Chapter 2, I appliquéd the petal onto the background. The edge of the outer (convex) curve of the petal is turned under. The curve is gentle enough that the seam allowance turns under easily. It is also my first instinct to appliqué the smaller piece onto the larger piece.

The curve on this flower petal piece (prepared for an orange version of the *Blue Daisy* project) is still gentle enough to easily be turned over.

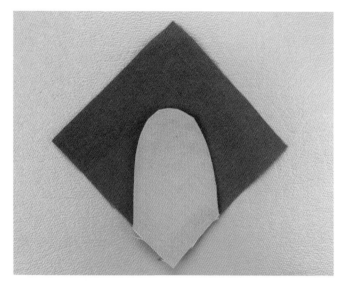

In this case, it made sense to turn over the edge on the curve and stitch the smaller piece on top of the larger piece.

There are times, however, when it makes more sense to appliqué the larger layer onto the smaller piece. In these cases, the inner (concave) curve of the background fabric will be turned under. This is the best option if the curve is dramatic, since tight outer curves can be more difficult to turn under. This is also a good technique to use if you want the smaller piece to recede slightly.

In this case, because the inner (concave) seam allowance is being turned, it needs to be clipped so that it can smoothly fold around the edge.

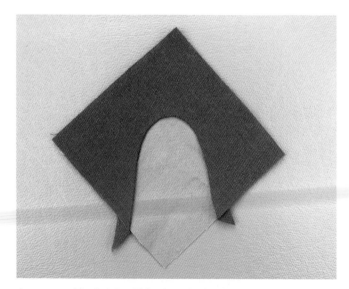

Compare this finished block with the finished block above. The curve is smoother, and the orange piece is less pronounced.

Turning Pointed Edges

The first decision you need to make with pointy shapes is which piece of fabric needs to be appliquéd on top of the other. Once that is decided, you will know how to proceed next. Pointy shapes show up in leaves, hair, whiskers, and beaks, among other things.

Option 1—Turn Under the Outer Point

For shapes that have points that are not super sharp, I usually appliqué the smaller convex piece onto the background fabric. The only tricky aspect is dealing with the extra triangular dog-ear created when two contiguous seam allowances are turned under.

Instead of trimming off the dog-ear, fold it back on itself. If the angle is not steep, the extra fabric can be hidden behind the appliqué using only one fold. Dab a bit of starch, starch alternative, or glue from a glue stick on the fold, and then iron it to hold it in place. If a little bit of the dog-ear is still visible from the front, use

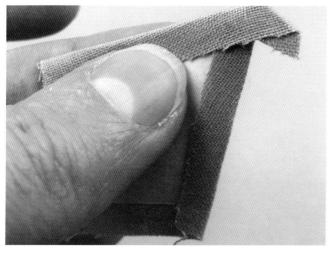

The extra dog-eared fabric left after turning a point can be tricky to correct.

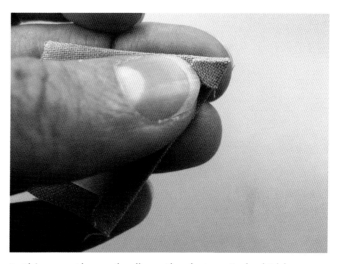

In this case, the angle allows the dog-ear to be hidden snugly behind the piece to be appliquéd.

Why can't you just cut off the extra dog-ear? Because that extra fabric keeps the appliqué piece from shredding while machine appliquéing. Without the dog-ear, the piece doesn't have enough structural stability to withstand a needle repeatedly piercing that close to the edge of the fabric.

This finished piece with the folded tip can now be appliquéd to the top of the base fabric.

For this square, the small fold visible at the top left of the yellow point can be pushed under the appliqué with a stiletto as it is being stitched.

Option 2—Turn Under the Inner Edges

When turning under the inner corner seam allowances, make sure to clip from the inner corner edge of the fabric to the inner corner edge of the freezer paper template. The tricky part in this technique is getting a sharp corner since the seam allowances can be quite narrow close to the inner point. I often use a stiletto to help guide the fabric while I iron it in place.

Inside corners are like concave curves—remember to cut the seam allowance from the edge of the fabric to the edge of the freezer paper template so each side can be turned over.

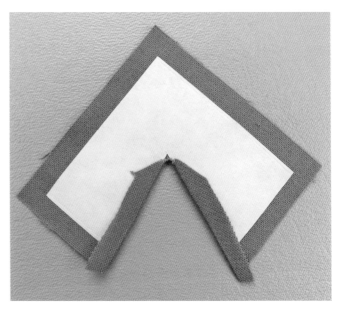

The cut at the corner allows the fabric edges to fold over the template and create the correct point angle.

The point is defined on the finished piece, which is ready to be appliquéd to the yellow base fabric.

I turned under the inner edges to create sharp points for the hair in my self portrait quilt, *I Woke Up Like This* (full quilt shown on page 17).

Tips for Extra-Sharp Points

Extra-sharp points are the trickiest of tricky blocks. You can use either of the first two options for making them, but there are a few things to keep in mind. Using option 1 requires folding the longer dog-ear more than once to hide it behind the appliqué and using a stiletto to push the seam allowances into place behind the appliqué piece while stitching. Using option 2 will be more difficult with narrow sharp points because the edges will get quite narrow as the edges get closer to the inner point.

OPTION 1

If you use option 1, you will have a longer dog-ear of extra fabric to hide behind the appliqué piece.

OPTION 2

If you use option 2, clipping the inner corner will help, but the edges will still be very narrow.

If this seems too fiddly, there is a third option that is by far my favorite way to deal with pointy blocks. For me, it's much less frustrating than trying to turn small, fussy edges like those in options 1 and 2. The technique is reminiscent of how paper piecing blocks are designed, breaking up spaces to make complicated shapes easy to sew with only straight lines.

OPTION 3

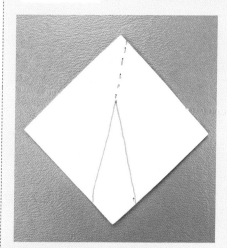

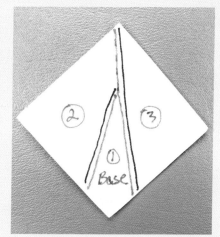

1. Draw the point shape on the shiny side of the freezer paper, continuing one of the straight lines off the edge of the square. In this example, I used a dotted line. I have now created a block made of three pieces, rather than the two pieces used in options 1 and 2.

2. On the dull paper side of the square, map out a plan of attack. Here I made the pink point (piece 1) the base layer and decided to add pieces on top of it. Piece 2 is marked with a red line where one of its edges needs to be turned under. Its second edge will tuck beneath piece 3's turned-edge side.

3. Prepare the individual shapes as usual and appliqué them onto the base layer. This technique creates an extra seam line, but I think that having an accurate, sharp point made with minimal fuss is worth it.

Island Pieces with Multiple Layers

Some blocks, like the ear in *Cheeky Chicken* (Block #27), have layers that are islands where all the edges need to be turned under. In this case, there is a white base layer, a red second layer, and a white oval piece for the ear that will go on top of

The white oval ear on this block from the *Cheeky Chicken* photo template will require a slightly different technique.

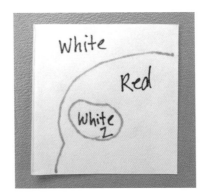

The oval labeled "White 2" is the ear. Since it is on its own, I will treat it as its own layer, rather than cutting it out of the red piece.

TIP: Sometimes it is easier to keep track of different layers by using a new piece of freezer paper for each layer, rather than using one piece to create a mask. When in doubt, use multiple pieces of freezer paper and label them accordingly.

1.

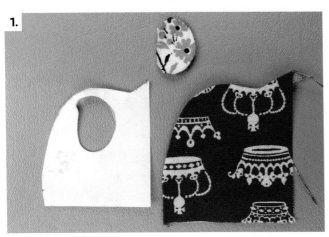

1. Turn the curved edge of the red appliqué piece first. Then remove the template from the red piece and cut out the white ear shape from the same freezer paper template. Prepare the ear for appliqué.

2.

2. Use the adjusted freezer paper template as a mask to determine the placement of the ear. Place the mask **shiny side up** on top of the right side of the red fabric. (It will have lost much of its shine since it's already been stuck down once, but you can reuse it.) Only the edges along the perimeter of the block need to have seam allowances

3.

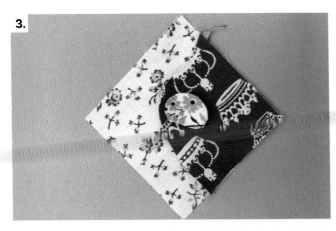

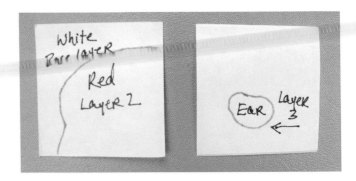

3. Layer the pieces to create the finished block, then appliqué and remove any extra fabric. The mask can be used as often as needed to align the "island" piece as you work on the block.

Tiny Pieces—Appliqué or Ignore?

Block #20 on the *Cheeky Chicken* photo template has a tiny red piece in the bottom corner. I decided not to put it in the quilt. The finished quilt has a little divot in the hen's comb, but I bet if I hadn't pointed it out, you would not have noticed. If I were to make this quilt again, I might add in the little red triangle. There is no logic to whether I decide to add in tiny pieces or not. It depends on my mood when I am working on a particular square and how detailed I feel like being. If the divots bother you, add in the small pieces. If you are tired of playing with tiny pieces, leave them out.

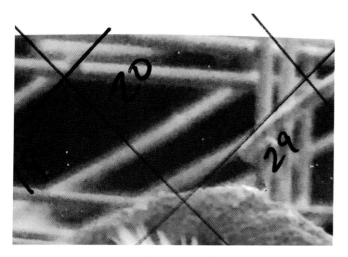 

I chose to leave out the tiny piece of red in the bottom corner of Block 20, leaving a small but barely noticeable divot in the hen's comb—these small style decisions are entirely up to you!

Tension Headaches

Ideally, for general sewing and quilting, you only want to see the stitched top thread on the top of the piece and the bobbin thread on the back of the piece, with no extra threads peeking through from the opposite side. For machine appliqué, I pull my bobbin thread tighter than I normally would and loosen my top thread, to ensure that the bobbin thread does not pop through to the top. The only downside to making these adjustments is that I need to remember to adjust the tension back to regular settings before I work on another project.

Most problems with stitch quality are often a simple fix. If you are experiencing problems, try the following before contacting your local machine repairperson:

- Take out the top thread completely and re-thread the machine.
- Pull out the bobbin and brush out any lint and loose threads. Check that the bobbin is inserted correctly and make sure that you have the correct bobbin for the machine you are using. Bobbins are not universal.
- Put a new needle into the machine.
- Oil the bobbin case. (Consult your manual to see if this is appropriate for your machine.)
- Wind a new bobbin and try the new one.
- Test the stitching with different spools of thread or flip the spool you are using so the thread moving through the machine is coming off the other end of the spool.

CHAPTER 5:
Projects

Clockwise from top left, *Cheeky Cat*, *Charming Chicken*, *Bearded Iris*, and *Dashing Dog*.

The four projects in this chapter are included in order of difficulty. The coloring of the *Cheeky Cat* is clear-cut, which makes it the easiest project to start with. The *Bearded Iris* is the most challenging, not because the construction is hard, but because it is the largest quilt with the greatest number of squares to keep track of. Each of the four projects has tips included in the instructions that carry through to the other projects, so it would be helpful to skim through all the projects before getting started.

My favorite stitched mosaic quilts to make are of animals since each animal has its own personality, and I get to know each individual as I work on them. I am superstitious about making eyes, though. The eyes are the last blocks I make, as they are the one element that really brings personality to these two-dimensional quilts. It is the little bit of reflection in the eye, called a catchlight, that pulls everything together. Until the catchlight is added at the very end of the construction, the animal looks flat, but once the catchlight is applied, ta-da! The animal comes to life. As you work, have faith that your quilt will animate and come to life as soon as you add in the small details like catchlights or sewn

Cheeky Cat

Cheeky Cat—Finished quilt
17" x 17" (43.2 x 43.2cm)

Thumper is the sweetest cat I have ever owned. Her sister, the
inspiration for *The Queen of Calico* (page 9), loved to have her photo
taken. No matter how many times I try to capture the beauty marks
on Thumper's cheeks, she only allows her photo to be taken on her
own terms. There is something about Thumper's quiet confidence
that commands respect. I make sure to honor her boundaries while

FABRIC AND PAPER REQUIREMENTS

- 2½" (6.4cm) squares of assorted fabrics, approximately:
  - 45 dark pink squares (for background)
  - 30 white squares (for white fur)
  - 60 black squares (for black fur and features)
  - 2 black and white striped squares (for whiskers)
  - 2 light pink squares (for nose)
  - 6 green squares (for eyes)
- 23" x 23" (58.4 x 58.4cm) batting
- 23" x 23" (58.4 x 58.4cm) backing fabric
- 1 scrap of double-sided fusible interfacing (for white catchlight in eye)
- Two 2¼" (5.7cm) WOF (width-of-fabric) strips for binding
- Fifty-five 2" (5.1cm) squares of freezer paper
- A copy of the cat photo on page 114 enlarged by 248% so that the photo prints at 18" x 18" (45.7 x 45.7cm)

My inspiration, Thumper, can be difficult to photograph, but the result is always worth it.

Choosing Fabrics

Since the colors and shapes are clearly defined in the original photo, there are not many decisions that need to be made to figure out the nuances of color or value gradations in this quilt. Pick some blacks, whites, and a background color and you're ready to go! But if you need a little more guidance or want to know my thought process as I made this sweet quilt, keep reading.

Dark Pink—I wanted this quilt to have a bit of a pop art feeling to it, so I did not vary the background coloration much. The saturated magenta contrasts nicely with the black and white, allowing the main focus of the image to pop. Although it was not consciously planned, magenta also complements Thumper's green eyes perfectly. The project would work just as well with a softer, more subtle background, as long as the background is lighter in value than the black of the cat's fur.

Black—Most of the black fabrics are very dark. A few have some white printing on them, but for the most part, I wanted to keep the black highly saturated. Since Thumper has some errant white hairs in square #37, I used a fabric that has a little bit of silver metallic details to literally and figuratively give her some sparkle.

White—Many of the white squares have a little visual texture to give the feeling of fur and untidiness. In the shadowed areas, such as the back of the neck, I used light gray fabrics rather than true white to capture the shadow. In places where the black and white fur mixes together, let the fabric do the work for you. Block #27 is mostly

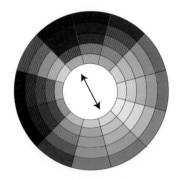

I lucked into using two complementary colors with this quilt. The color wheel shows why the magenta background works so well with Thumper's green eyes.

white, but I fussy cut the square so that the black marks would follow the same direction as where Thumper's white and black hairs mix.

Green—For Thumper's eyes, my goal was to add movement and some light areas to enhance the natural shimmer. The largest green pieces are small-scale foliage prints, which I usually wouldn't have thought of to use in eyes. They turned out to have the right amount of texture and movement to help the eyes come alive.

Light Pink—Thumper has asymmetrical markings on her nose. The two small pieces of light pink help to distinguish her nose and lip from the rest of her features.

Construction

1. Prepare the photo as described in Chapter 1. If there are any shapes in the photo that need clarification, use your

TIP: Don't worry about capturing every strand of fur; just outline the general fluffiness. Individual hairs can be added in later during the quilting or embroidery process.

2. Audition the background arrangement of squares by pinning the fabric to the grid of the photo (remember to pin the photo on foam core).

3. Once you are happy with the arrangement, do the same with the white and black squares.

At this point, if you need to use a light box to trace your image onto the freezer paper squares, you will realize that you can't move the photo to the light box unless you remove the fabric and the dozens of pins attaching it to the foam core board. To get around this problem, I've created a numbered grid drawn on a piece of foam core that I can transfer the pinned fabrics to until I am ready to use them. It is propped up against a wall in my workspace. As I pull the fabric off the photo grid, I pin it to the corresponding numbered box on the plain, numbered grid. It is not pretty, but it is lightweight and easy to pin into. You could also draw boxes on a piece of batting or paper, or even label each piece of fabric individually—whatever you have handy that will work best in your space.

4. Prepare the blocks and machine appliqué any squares that need to be stitched. For more information on basic construction see Chapter 3.

5. Sew the squares together in diagonal rows. Then sew the rows together.

6. Layer the top on the batting and backing.

7. Quilt as desired. See suggestions on page 88 and Chapter 6 for more details.

8. Square up and trim all the layers. My quilt is trimmed to about 17" x 17" (43.2 x 43.2cm).

Notice how the colors and patterns of the fabric choices for Thumper's eyes, nose, and mouth area help to distinguish these features from the rest of the face and create energy and personality.

Tips for Tricky Elements

There are a few details in this quilt that might be trickier or require special techniques or guidance. Here are a few tips to make things easier.

Whiskers—Blocks #17 & #39

Thumper has spectacular long white whiskers, which show up beautifully against her black coat. To mimic the whiskers' upward trajectory over her eyes, I added in some black and white striped pieces. These are not literal representations of the whiskers, but they give an impression of the whiskers. See Quilting Suggestions on the right for more information on including the whiskers.

Catchlight in the Eyes

I am a big fan of turned-edge appliqué, but even I know when to stop being a purist and use other tools available to me, especially on itty-bitty pieces. I added the white catchlights for this quilt by using small pieces of double-sided fusible interfacing. If you prefer to stitch the catchlight in rather than using raw-edge appliqué, you can add it either by hand or by machine stitching. (See Eye—Block #28 on page 92 for photos of this process as used for the *Charming Chicken* project.)

1. Iron a small piece of double-sided fusible interfacing to the back side of the catchlight fabric. Keep the heat on just enough for the interfacing to stick. If the interfacing gets too hot, it releases and does not stick at all. Follow the manufacturer's directions on the packaging for the correct temperature.

2. Cut out the shape of the catchlight. You can either trace the shape on a piece of freezer paper or guesstimate the size.

3. If the interfacing has a paper backing, peel it off, and place the catchlight on the eye. Since these pieces are very small, tweezers can be a helpful tool in placing the piece in the right location. I estimate the placement, then take a photo of the whole quilt to confirm that the location is correct.

4. Iron in place.

5. Anchor the catchlight in place with monofilament or matching thread.

Quilting Suggestions

I used white 40 wt. 100% cotton thread to add a few details with the quilting stitch. The white highlight in Block #36 and the long whiskers are stitched in. Each of these details was too small to appliqué, but a few stitches give dimension and shape to the face (and to the quilt as a whole).

Quilt Layout Diagram

Charming Chicken

For my birthday a few years ago, I asked my family to go with me to the Northeastern Poultry Congress so that I could take photos of chickens. My family is very accommodating, and they tolerated a few hours of bird gawking. I learned that professional show chickens really know how to pose for photos, and this hen was no exception. While the hen looks great, the background behind her is cluttered. In this quilt project, ignore the agricultural center background and replace it with pretty fabrics so you can show off your own show chicken.

Charming Chicken—Finished quilt
17" x 17" (43.2 x 43.2cm)

FABRIC AND PAPER REQUIREMENTS

- 2½" (6.4cm) squares of assorted fabrics, approximately:
  - 53 blue-green squares (for background)
  - 22 white squares (for feathers)
  - 20 black squares (for feathers and pupil)
  - 10 black and white squares (for feathers)
  - 11 red squares (for wattle and comb)
  - 2 dark red squares (for wattle)
  - 3 light red squares (for wattle)
  - 1 pink square (for above the eye)
  - 2 brown squares (for eye)
  - 4 yellow-orange squares (for beak)
- 23" x 23" (58.4 x 58.4cm) batting
- 23" x 23" (58.4 x 58.4cm) backing fabric
- Two 2¼" (5.7cm) WOF (width-of-fabric) strips for binding
- Ninety 2" (5.1cm) squares of freezer paper
- A copy of the hen photo on page 116 enlarged by 248% so that the photo prints at 18" x 18" (45.7 x 45.7cm)

The background in the photo that inspired this project is cluttered, so I edited out those extra background details in the finished design.

Choosing Fabrics

The hen includes some clear colors: reds, whites, and blacks. For the background, I went with a blue-green that would contrast with the main focus of the hen. For more insight into my color choices, keep reading.

Blue-Green—The blue-green background helps the red of the hen's comb stand out. Even though the background isn't a strict green, there is enough green in the fabrics to complement the red. Complementary colors always like to show off when they are next to each other, and these two are no exception. Notice that there are a variety of blue-greens in a range of values. Some of the squares are dark teal while others are pale seafoam. The variation in value encourages the viewer's eye to move across the quilt, but more importantly, the range of values helps the chicken stand out against the background. The white of the hen stands out against the dark blue-greens, while the black feathers are stark against the lighter blue-greens. Placing light next to dark creates a defined edge between the chicken and the background. Since the hen is the star, she should stand out and shine on her own.

Black—The squares in my black section are not all black. Many have white in them, others are navy blue, but they all read as very dark. You should choose fabrics for these squares that are at least 75% dark.

Black and white—These are transition squares. They mimic the black and white feathers in the chicken and

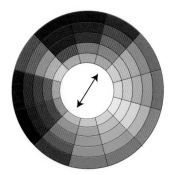

For this quilt, I actively used the color wheel to pick a background color that would be complementary to the red of the hen's comb, making it pop!

help move the viewer's eye from the white head to the black tail feathers without creating harsh visual lines. A good rule of thumb for the black and white squares is to choose fabrics that are approximately half dark and half light.

White—The "white" squares in this hen are not actually white at all. Even though our brains tell us that this is a white and black chicken, on closer inspection, she is more of an off-white and black bird. The fabrics at the head are lighter in value than those along the back, mimicking the ombré coloring of the bird. Let the prints in the fabrics read as feather texture. The more fabrics you use that can visually act as feathers, the less work with appliqué or quilting embellishments you'll have.

Red and Pink—The difficult part about the wattle and comb is that the folds and crevices are hard to capture. Rather than trying to recreate all the undulations, focus on a few key folds. This is a case of less is more—don't stress about the details, let the viewers' eyes and brains fill them in.

Construction

1. Prepare the photo as described in Chapter 1. If there are any shapes on the photo that need clarification, use your black marker to define the edges of the hen and the background. It is easier to clarify these distinctions before you start pinning fabric to the picture.

2. Audition the background fabric arrangement by pinning the fabric within the grid of the photo (remember to pin the photo on foam core).

3. Once you are happy with the arrangement, do the same with the white and black squares.

4. Prepare the blocks and machine appliqué any squares that need to be stitched. For more information on basic construction, see Chapter 3.

5. Sew the squares together in diagonal rows. Then sew the rows together.

6. Layer the top on the batting and backing.

7. Quilt as desired. See suggestions below and Chapter 6 for more details.

8. Square up and trim all the layers. My quilt is trimmed to about 17" x 17" (43.2 x 43.2cm).

9. Bind and label the quilt. See Chapter 6 for more details.

For this quilt, I drew a line along the hen's back and another on her chest since those edges visually blend into the background in the photo.

TIP: Step back and look at the whole composition or take a photo and look at it on your screen. Is the chicken well-defined and distinct from the background? Do the colors move in a way you like? Adjust the squares as necessary. Sometimes moving one or two squares will be just enough to help the arrangement sing.

Tips for Tricky Elements

There are a few details in this quilt that might be trickier or require special techniques or guidance. Here are a few tips to make things easier.

Wattle—Block #50

At first look, this block seems complicated because of the different reds and the ripples in the wattle. In my block, I used only three different red fabrics and did not try to mimic every shadow. The key to creating the appearance of folds is to use reds with slightly different values, placing the lightest red in between the two darker reds. The light red is the backside of a commercial fabric. I liked the texture and

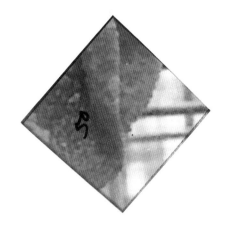

Remember that the easiest way to work with complicated blocks is to use a cardstock frame to block out the surrounding information.

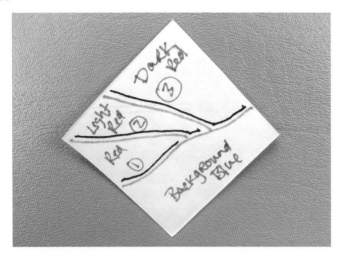

For my freezer paper template, I labeled each section with detailed notes to keep things clear and organized.

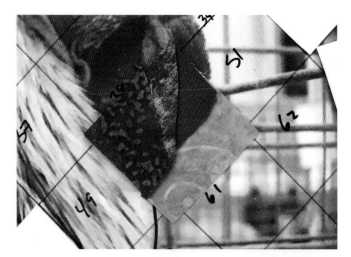

This final combination of fabrics gives a good impression of the wattle's texture without having to appliqué a ton of tiny details.

Eye—Block #28

Eyes are the most important part of any portrait. If the eye doesn't look right, you have lost the audience's trust that you can make a portrait. Fortunately, birds' eyes are small and not complicated to make.

The entire hen's eye is within Block #28, but there are other elements in this block, as well, including the comb and white feathers.

1.

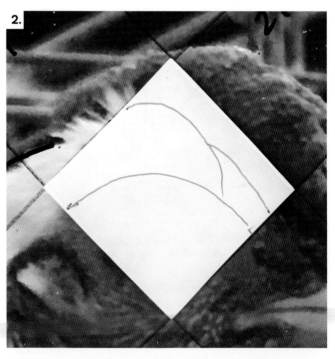

The eye block includes a few different elements that may seem complicated at first but breaking it down into simpler pieces will make this block more approachable.

1. Determine the individual fabric pieces needed and the order in which to layer them. I used one piece of freezer paper to draw out everything except the eyeball. I used the red comb as the base layer.

2.

2. Draw the basic shapes in Block #28 on the **SHINY** side of a piece of freezer paper. Rather than appliquéing every spikey feather above the eye, I approximated the overall

3.

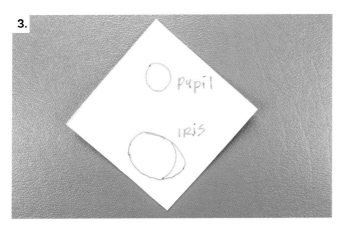

3. Because the eye is a separate "island" made up of multiple pieces, you need to create separate templates for those pieces. Notice that the iris is made up of two pieces: a piece for the actual brown color of the iris and a piece meant to represent the conjunctiva (or white) around the iris, which appears reddish pink on this hen.

4.

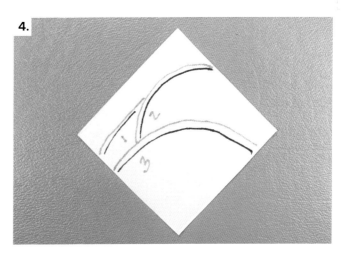

4. Remember to make any notes to yourself on the **PAPER SIDE** of the freezer paper square.

5.

5. Prepare to appliqué by turning under your edges and gluing the base block pieces in place. See Chapter 3 for specific details.

6.

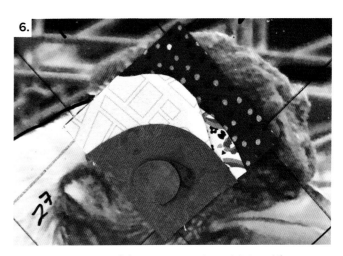

6. Prepare the iris of the eye using the additional freezer paper template.

7.

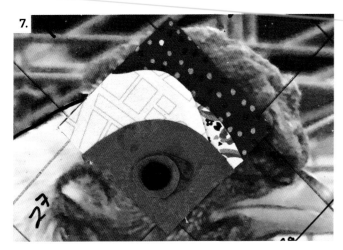

7. Add the pupil piece on top of the iris pieces, glue them all in place, and machine appliqué all the pieces down to the base layer.

8.

8. Hand stitch a few small stitches of white thread where the catchlight appears in the photo. I used a double strand of 50 wt. cotton thread. Notice how much livelier the eye looks as soon as the "light in the eye" is added!

The finished block has a few quilted elements that add interest, but it's the hand-stitched eye light that truly brings this eye block, and by extension, the entire quilt, to life.

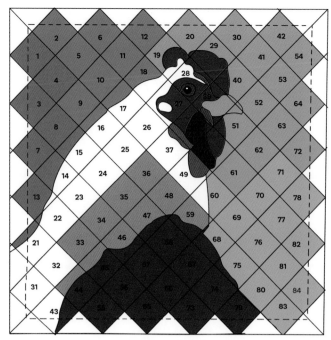

Quilt Layout Diagram

Quilting Suggestions

Poultry feathers are fun to quilt because they are organic, have movement, and do not need to be precise. I quilted feather shapes in the body of the hen, occasionally quilting into the background to mimic a flyaway feather.

Quilting can also be used to add details that are too challenging to appliqué. Here I added in the crease around the eye and beak with the quilting line.

In the finished quilt top, the red quilted crease lines add some much-needed definition without overpowering the eye itself.

Dashing Dog

Sarge is a classic mutt. He is handsome, friendly, loves to go for hikes, and is a ball of energy. He is also well loved by my sister-in-law and her family. Now that he is twelve years old, Sarge is starting to slow down a bit, but not much. The beauty of Sarge's shape is that he has a classic dog silhouette, so this pattern can be used to make a dog of any color.

I had a few challenges with the background color and design for this quilt. I solved my color problem using the color wheel (see page 96), but I also needed a solution for the negative space to the right of Sarge's nose. As I

Dashing Dog—Finished quilt
32" x 25" (81.3 x 63.5cm)

worked, I realized that if I trimmed up that side of the quilt through blocks 80, 98, 104, etc., his nose would get cut off. To give his nose a little space to breathe, I added an additional blue square to every row. These are represented on the illustration on page 119 as lettered squares: A, B, C, etc. If you find that your dog needs even more space, add additional squares to each row until the composition feels right to you.

FABRIC AND PAPER REQUIREMENTS

- 2½" (6.4cm) squares of assorted fabrics, approximately:
    - 85 dark blue squares (for background)
    - 40 white squares (for snout, neck, and teeth)
    - 45 light to medium orange-brown squares (for fur)
    - 18 dark brown squares (for ears and eye)
    - 20 dark gray and black squares (for gums, nose, and eye)
    - 4 pink and purple squares (for tongue)
    - 4 red squares (for collar)
- Three 1½" (3.8cm) white WOF (width-of-fabric) strips for inner border
- Four 3½" (8.9cm) dark blue WOF (width-of-fabric) strips for outer border
- 38" x 32" (96.5 x 81.3cm) batting
- 38" x 32" (96.5 x 81.3cm) backing fabric
- 1 scrap of double-sided fusible interfacing (for white catchlight in eye)
- Four 2¼" (5.7cm) WOF (width-of-fabric) strips for binding
- Sixty-five 2" (5.1cm) squares of freezer paper
- A copy of the dog photo on page 118 enlarged by 331% so that the photo prints at 24" x 18" (61 x 45.7cm)

Because Sarge has such a classic dog silhouette, you can use the original photo to make universally appealing dog quilts in a multitude of colors.

Choosing Fabrics

To be honest, I struggled a bit with color when I started working on this project. Most of the time I spend with Sarge is in his lush backyard, so I started by placing a green background behind him like in the original photo. But the green did not do him any justice and led to a flat, dull arrangement. After a few days of giving the piece the side-eye while it hung on my design wall, I consulted my trusty color wheel and started over. Since Sarge's fur is quite orange, I tested the complement to that—blue—for the background. As soon as I started pinning blue blocks to the design wall, Sarge came to life. Nothing else about the composition had changed—that is the power of color.

My first background concept was green. It felt flat to me, so I went back to the drawing board with my color wheel to solve the problem.

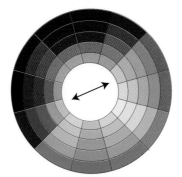

To liven up Sarge's orange fur, I ended up changing the background to a complementary color: blue.

Orange-Browns and Dark Brown—If Sarge were a person, we would say he's a strawberry blonde—not quite a redhead, not quite a blonde. As I dug through my beige and brown fabrics, I looked for fabrics that had orange undertones to mimic his reddish coat. In a few places, the fabrics even have a green undertone. Those fabrics went into the shadows under his ear to give the piece a little more depth.

Dark Gray and Black—Since dog noses and mouths are wet and have a sheen to them, I used mottled fabrics. That small amount of visual texture is enough to give the nose and mouth the feeling of life. There is also no need to include every fold and crevice in these parts. A few clues given to the viewer, such as the hint of a dark nostril in Block #104, is enough for them to fill in the rest of the shape. The most difficult part of choosing nose fabrics was making sure that the nose and the background had enough visual distinction. The nose needed to be dark enough and the blue behind it needed to be light enough to create value contrast between both. I am not sure I was completely successful. If I were to make this quilt again, I would rectify this issue by adding a section of lighter blues around the nose.

White—Aim for some true white squares for the snout and then transition the color to more beige and light-brown squares as you move closer to the cheek. Every quilt I make has things that make me laugh stitched into them. They are my own personal jokes. Square #86 is that piece in this quilt. It has dogs printed

on it, and even though the color isn't perfect, the subject matter is, so I left it in.

Red—Rather than replicating the collar exactly, I gave Sarge a red collar to make it stand out. I also fused an *S* onto the collar in blocks #71 and #82. Remember that

When you start creating your stitched mosaic quilts, remember to think of small details you can add to personalize each quilt. In this case, I hid some funny dog fabric in my dog quilt! The color wasn't a perfect fit, but it was close enough, and I loved hiding this little easter egg within the larger quilt.

Construction

1. Prepare the photo as described in Chapter 1. If there are any shapes in the photo that need clarification, use your black marker to define the edges between the dog and the background.

2. Audition the blue background squares by pinning the fabric to the grid of the photo (remember to pin the photo on foam core).

3. Once you are happy with the arrangement, do the same with the white and brown squares.

4. Prepare the blocks and machine appliqué any squares that need to be stitched. For more information on basic construction see Chapter 3.

5. Sew the squares together in diagonal rows. Then sew the rows together. **Note:** this quilt has a border, so the following steps are slightly different from those in the *Cheeky Cat* and *Charming Chicken* projects.

6. After pressing, square up the quilt top. My top was trimmed to 24¼" x 17" (61.6 x 43.2cm).

> **TIP:** Be very gentle with the quilt top after it is trimmed. The edges are now on the bias, meaning the diagonal grain of the fabric, and will stretch easily. If the edges do stretch a little, spray them with starch and iron them before you sew the borders on. This will help the fibers contract a bit and alleviate any flaring.

7. Cut two 1½" (3.8cm) white inner border strips to 24¼" (61.6cm). **Note:** The border measurements used here are those I cut for my quilt top. Measure your quilt top each time you add a set of borders and adjust your border length as needed. This will ensure that the borders fit your quilt exactly.

8. Pin these strips to the top and bottom of the quilt top and sew them on. Press the seam allowances toward the center of the quilt top.

9. Cut two 19" (48.3cm) strips from the remaining 1½" (3.8cm) white inner border strip.

Quilt Layout Diagram

10. Pin these strips to the sides of the quilt top and sew them on. Press the seam allowances toward the quilt top.

11. Cut two 3½" (8.9cm) blue outer border strips to 26¼" (66.7cm).

12. Pin the blue borders on the sides of the quilt top and inner border and sew them on. Press the seam allowances toward the outer blue border.

13. Cut two 3½" (8.9cm) blue outer border strips to 25" (63.5cm).

14. Pin these blue strips to the top and bottom and inner border of the quilt top and sew them on. Press the seam allowances toward the outer blue border.

15. Layer the completed top on the batting and backing.

16. Quilt as desired. See suggestions below and Chapter 6 for more details.

17. Square up and trim all the layers. My quilt is trimmed to about 32" x 25" (81.3 x 63.5).

Tips for Tricky Elements

There are a few details in this quilt that might be trickier or require special techniques or guidance. Here are a few tips to make things easier.

Eyes

Look closely at the original photo, and you may see that there are multiple catchlights in the dog's eye, some grayer than others. To mimic that, I used two different colors of fabrics, white and light gray, and applied them using raw-edge appliqué with fusible interfacing. (See Catchlight in the Eyes on page 88 for more details in the *Cheeky Cat* project and Eye—Block #28 on page 92 for photos of this process as used for the *Charming Chicken* project.)

Sometimes there will be a variety of tiny shapes and different shades of catchlights in the eye. For these very small details, I often use interfacing and different fabric colors for raw-edge appliqué.

Teeth—Blocks #94, #101, and #102

Teeth are my least favorite feature to replicate. They can be fiddly. Since the dog is smiling and most of his teeth are hidden under his tongue and gums, I only made the distinctive eyeteeth, which are in blocks #94, #101, and #102. Our brains know that the rest of his teeth are there and will fill in the details for us.

Teeth can be tricky. For this quilt, I've edited the blocks to include only the necessary details and I've left the rest for the viewers' brains to fill in.

Quilting Suggestions

In this quilt, I quilted in loose lines that follow the direction of the fur, just enough to give the impression of hair. I also stitched in his white eyelashes. Adding in that small detail pulled the whole quilt together for me. I freehand quilted the background and outer border with swirls to symbolize Sarge's energy and to give the background movement. I anchored down the inner border by stitching in the ditch.

Bearded Iris

Irises are such a lovely sign of late spring, at least in New England, where I live. Once the irises arrive, I feel like summer is on its way, and I can start thinking about spending more time outside in the sun. This project is a good example of how, even when replicating a photo, there are still design decisions to be made before starting to sew. The first thing I needed to decide was how many of the iris buds and leaves to include in the quilt. Including everything seemed tedious, and the extra foliage did not serve the large iris bloom, which

*Bearded Iris—*Finished quilt
29" x 43" (73.7 x 1.1m)

is the star of the show. I decided to keep the blooming iris, two small buds, and the leaves attached to them. I considered adding in more leaves since I felt the quilt could use more green along the bottom of the piece, but in the end, I added a green inner border instead. The border literally frames the piece and adds that bit of extra green without also adding unnecessary details.

FABRIC AND PAPER REQUIREMENTS

- 2½" (6.4cm) squares of assorted fabrics, approximately:
    - 180 yellow squares (for background)
    - 42 lighter medium purple squares (for upright petals)
    - 45 dark purple squares (for buds and downward petals)
    - 25 white squares (for papery sheathing around buds)
    - 40 green squares (for stems and leaves)
    - 5 orange squares (for beards)
- Three 1" (2.5cm) green WOF (width-of-fabric) strips for inner border (if WOF is less than 42" [1.1m], cut four strips)
- Four 4½" (11.4cm) purple WOF (width-of-fabric) strips for outer border
- 34" x 48" (86.4cm x 1.2m) batting
- 34" x 48" (86.4cm x 1.2m) backing fabric
- Five 2¼" (5.7cm) WOF (width-of-fabric) strips for binding
- Eighty 2" (5.1cm) squares of freezer paper
- A copy of the iris photo on page 120 enlarged by 400% so that the photo prints at 24" x 36" (61 x 91.4cm)

Once I started working on this project, I decided I didn't like the proportion of iris to background in the original photo. The iris needed to feel taller and thinner, so I narrowed the final quilt by cropping off some of each side of the photo and a row on the bottom. In the illustration on page 121, the red line indicates the edge of the iris panel in the finished quilt. While trying to decide where to crop the piece, I pinned a piece of twill tape on the photo where I considered cropping the image. The tape allowed me to experiment with the proportions without committing to any changes until I knew for sure what I wanted to do. A ribbon, yarn, or washi tape would work as well for mocking up the sample.

I used twill tape pinned to my prepared photo to test out different options for cropping the image. Use twill tape, ribbon, yarn, or washi tape to easily and temporarily experiment with proportions early in the process.

I chose to remove some of the buds and leaves in the original photo from the finished quilt design to allow the iris bloom to stand out.

Choosing Fabrics

The main colors for this quilt were really dictated by the natural colors of the iris and the color wheel. For a little more guidance, or if you want to know my thought process as I made this lovely spring quilt, keep reading.

Yellow—Since irises have such bright, happy summer connotations for me, I wanted to put my iris on a yellow background. Yellow is also purple's complementary color, so I went with my first instinct and stuck with yellow. I started out with pale light yellows and found that the piece needed darker, more mustardy yellows toward the bottom to ground it. The strong, darker yellows at the base of the quilt do not have much value contrast with the green leaves, but I like how they feel earthier. It can be hard to find a wide variety of yellow fabrics in quilt shops. It is not a color that quilters usually gravitate towards or purchase unless they need it for a specific project. When I find a "good yellow"—one that is

TIP: If you are undecided on whether to use a fabric, audition the fabric with others in the piece. Remove the fabric you're unsure about. If you miss it, put it back in. If you don't miss it, set it aside. I definitely missed the ombré border when I moved it away from the iris! That's how I knew it needed to be part of the quilt.

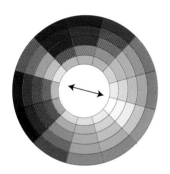

Purples and yellows are on opposite sides of the color wheel—and you can never go wrong using complementary colors!

Dark and Light Purple—Batiks turned out to be ideal fabrics to give the impression of the slightly transparent quality of the flower's petals. They mimic the veining without allowing the viewer's eye to get stuck looking at any one pattern. I used light purples and violets for the upper petals (the standards). I reserved the dark purples for the downturned petals (the falls) and the buds. I had to restrain myself from adding in too many extra details trying to replicate the layering in the petals. Less is more, in this case. The purple ombré outer border added an element to the quilt that surprised me. The light centers of each border seem to glow, in turn helping the iris itself shine. Thankfully, a friend had this ombré fabric in her stash, and she generously shared it with me.

Orange—The iris in the photo has yellow and white beards. (Mother Nature knows the colors—like yellow and purple—that work well together!) Since I chose yellow as a base, yellow beards would not work for me—they would fade into the background. I made my beards orange and white so they would still be a warm color but would show up on the yellow background.

White—Until I started writing this, I had no idea that the white, papery sheathing around iris buds is

called a spathe. Obviously, I am not an avid gardener. The spathes were great fun to pick fabrics for, though. I chose fabrics that were mostly white, but also included some purple and pink in them to represent the purple bud wrapped inside. Although you might not recognize it, there is even part of a snail on one of the pieces—another hidden fabric joke I included because it made me laugh.

Green—Remember when I mentioned that I planned on using a green background for the *Dashing Dog* project but changed my mind? The dog's loss is the iris's gain. The green fabrics here were originally intended to be behind Sarge, but they work perfectly with the iris. Keep any 2½" (6.4cm) square you cut and don't

Choosing white fabrics with pinks and purples allowed me to give the impression of hidden buds beneath papery spathes and gave me an opportunity to hide part of a flowery snail in my quilt.

Construction

1. Prepare the photo as described in Chapter 1. If there are any shapes in the photo that need clarification, use your black marker to define the edges between the flower and the background. Make any notes as to which stems and leaves you plan to include in the finished quilt.

2. Audition the background arrangement of squares by pinning the fabric to the grid of the photo (remember to pin the photo on foam core).

3. Once you are happy with the arrangement, do the same with the purple and green flower squares.

4. Prepare the blocks and machine appliqué any squares that need to be stitched. For more information on basic construction see Chapter 3.

5. Sew the squares together in diagonal rows. Then sew the rows together. **Note:** this quilt has a border, so the following steps are slightly different from those in the *Cheeky Cat* and *Charming Chicken* projects.

6. After pressing, square up the quilt top. My top was trimmed to 20" x 34" (50.8 x 86.4cm).

7. Cut two 1" (2.5cm) green inner border strips to 34" (86.4cm). **Note:** The border measurements used here are what I cut for my quilt top. Measure your quilt top each time you add a set of borders and adjust your border length as needed. This will ensure that the borders fit your quilt exactly.

8. Pin these strips to the sides of the quilt top and sew them on. Press the seam allowances toward the green border.

9. Cut two 1" (2.5cm) green inner border strips to 21" (53.3cm).

10. Pin these strips to the top and bottom of the quilt top and sew them on. Press the seam allowances toward the green border.

11. Cut two 4½" (11.4cm) purple outer border strips to 35" (88.9cm).

12. Pin the purple borders on the sides and inner border of the quilt top and sew them on. Press the seam allowances toward the green inner border.

13. Cut two 4½" (11.4cm) purple outer border strips to 29" (73.7cm).

14. Pin the purple borders to the top and bottom of the quilt top and inner border and sew them on. Press the seam allowances toward the green inner border.

15. Layer the completed top on the batting and backing.

16. Quilt as desired. See suggestions on page 103 and Chapter 6 for more details.

Tips for Tricky Elements

There are a few details in this quilt that might be trickier or require special techniques or guidance. Here are a few tips to make things easier.

Blocks #98 and #116

The most challenging part of these two blocks is deciding how much detail to add. Rather than trying to recreate each shadow and fold within the flower, I used printed fabrics that have a good deal of visual texture to mimic the fold in the petals.

In Block #98, purple was my base layer, then I added green and white. The green template had deep concave *U* shapes at the top that were tricky to turn under. For this piece, clip the seam allowances and press carefully. Or, if that is too tedious, ignore the *U* shapes entirely and make the whole top of the block green. No one will miss the purple accents. See my finished Block #98 on page

The pale purple accents at the top of Block #98 are the bottom of the large bloom above. They can easily be cropped out by making the top of the square green and the viewer will never notice that they're gone.

I used quilting and threads in different colors to build up the impression of dimension for the fluffy beards of the iris.

Quilting Suggestions

Since the petals have nebulous shapes that are hard to capture, I used the quilting line, rather than appliquéd shapes, to imitate the flowy motion and layering of the petals.

Adding filaments to the beards was the most important detail I added with the quilting. The quilting lines add texture and help define the characteristic caterpillar-like beards. I used two different orange threads to add in more color.

Quilt Layout Diagram

I chose to include these small purple details, as you can see in the purple and pink polka dot fabric on the finished square, but a simplified block would work just as well.

CHAPTER 6:
Quilting and Finishing

The first 15 years of my professional quilting life were spent as a longarm quilter, quilting other people's quilt tops for hire. Because of that experience, quilting is something that I think about throughout the life of a project, not just when the top is finished. As I piece and appliqué, I am always considering how quilting lines can enhance what I am working on. If a detail is too small to appliqué, or if a section will need a bit of definition or shadow, I think about how I might use thread to create that effect. While I am constructing a stitched mosaic piece, I am also aware that quilting can add texture

and dimension if needed. The quilted line is perfect for adding hair, feathers, wrinkles, or the stamen in a flower.

At this point in my life, I do not care to spend much time doing the actual quilting, as that's not the most fun part for me. Nor do I want to reinvent the wheel for each new piece. My goal is to add the quilting needed to get the desired results. If you look through the Gallery starting on page 8, you will see that I use the same quilting strategies in many of my stitched mosaic quilts.

All of that said, there is absolutely no reason you need to do any quilting other than putting on a walking foot and stitching in the ditch through the diagonal seam

General Quilting Steps

1. Stitch in the ditch around the main image and around any major shapes using monofilament thread. This stabilizes the layers of the quilt, while also sharpening the distinction between foreground and background. The monofilament helps add dimension to the piece without introducing any additional color elements.

2. Quilt the background. I often quilt a 1" (2.5cm) diagonal grid through the background. This is easy to do since the quilt already has a 2" (5.1cm) grid within it. Other times, I freehand quilt an all-over pattern, such as swirls or flowers. In these cases, I want the background to have a little motion without being fussy.

3. Free-motion quilt hair, fur, and feathers. When quilting in these details, I make the quilting lines generally move in the direction of the fur pattern of the animal. For example, when quilting a dog's neck, the lines follow the length of the neck rather than encircling it. Fur and feathers often extend into the background to add texture and a little dishevelment, much like real life. For this step, I may use monofilament thread, but I typically use a 40

wt. thread in a color that matches the fur or feathers. This is a good time to use variegated threads, which can help create color and movement.

4. Add in any details that need to be accentuated, such as the chicken's eye crease, the cat's whiskers, or to add a catchlight within an eye. I often use a 40 wt. colored thread for these details.

5. Add any additional quilting as needed. The density of quilting across the quilt should be even. If the background is tightly quilted, while the figure has just a few quilting lines, the quilt will be oddly puffy and may not hang straight. At one point, I thought I was finished with the quilting of my self-portrait *I Woke Up Like This* (page 17), but when I pulled back to look at it, it did not look correct. It took me a few days looking at the quilt to realize that the figure was too puffy. To solve the issue, I added contour lines to my face, which evened out the quilting density.

I thought that adding more lines to my face would make me look wrinkly, but it smoothed out the whole composition.

TIP: Do not cut off the triangular edges or square up the quilt top until after it is quilted unless you are adding borders before quilting. If you plan to add borders, see the discussions of borders in the *Dashing Dog* project on page 95 and the *Bearded Iris* project on page 99). Trimming off the triangles creates bias edges on the quilt top and makes it challenging to keep the edges from stretching.

Squaring Up

After quilting, you must trim off the jagged edges and square up the quilt.

1. Start with an upper corner and place the 45-degree line of a square quilting ruler directly on top of the seam that leads into the corner of the quilt.

2. Before trimming, check to see that the edges of the ruler are ¼" (6.4mm) beyond the finished diamond points.

3. Use a rotary cutter to square off the first corner. From that corner, trim up the quilt as you traditionally would. I line up multiple rulers to get a straight line. In an ideal world, all your outside diamond points will end up exactly ¼" (6.4mm) inside the cut line. I do not live in an ideal world, so mine rarely line up perfectly, and I usually lose some of the points of my diamonds. Because the blocks are on-point and there is plenty of visual stimulation in the whole piece, I find that any "imperfections" won't be

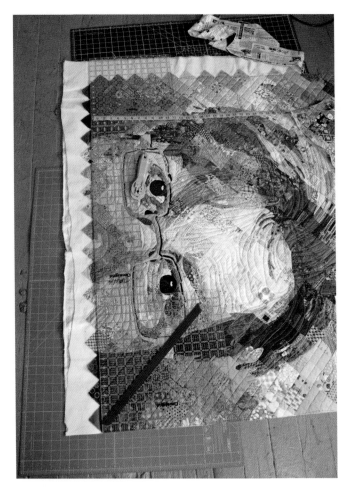

It can be very helpful to use multiple quilting rulers and measuring tapes while squaring up stitched mosaic quilts.

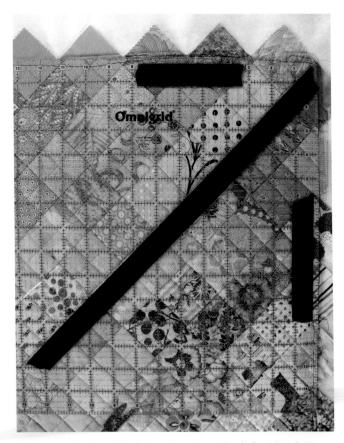

In this photo, the 45-degree line is on the left side of the blue painter's tape.

Batting

For quilts that are designed to hang on a wall, I use either a 100% cotton or a 70% cotton/30% polyester batting. These battings give the piece some heft and structure so that the quilt will hang nicely. My favorite batting to use for most quilts is 100% wool and several of my early stitched mosaic quilts have 100% wool batting in them. I found these early quilts to be "wiggly" and challenging to square up, so I began using batting made of other fibers for stitched mosaic quilts.

Binding

Binding is the final step in the quilting process, and it literally frames the quilt. There are many ways to bind a quilt, and they are all the "right" way to do it. The instructions below are how I bind my quilts, but use the method that works best for you.

For wall-hanging quilts, the first thing I do is stabilize the edges with ¼" (6.4mm) twill tape. The tape keeps

1. Measure the width and length of the quilt. I'll use the measurements of the *Dashing Dog* stitched mosaic quilt—32" x 25" (81.3 x 63.5cm)—as an example.

2. Cut two pieces of twill tape the width of the quilt: 32" (81.3cm).

3. Pin one piece of twill to the top edge and the other to the bottom edge of the backside of the quilt. Distribute

4. Stitch the tape to the top and bottom of the quilt, approximately ⅛" (3.2mm) inside the edge of the quilt.

5. Cut two pieces of twill tape the length of the quilt minus ½" (1.3cm): 25" - ½" = 24½" (63.5 - 1.3 = 62.2cm).

6. Pin one piece to each side of the back of the quilt. The twill tape ends will butt up against the tape at the top and bottom of the quilt.

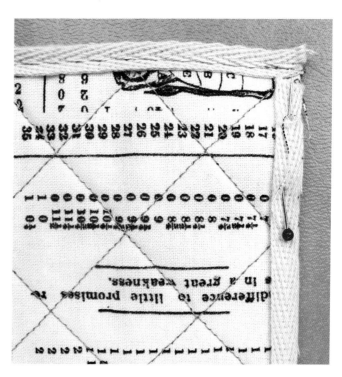

The twill tape and quilt bulk should be spread evenly across the quilt edge.

The twill tape for the side edges is cut ½" (1.3cm) shorter than the full length of the quilt to allow it to sit directly against the top and bottom twill tape rather than overlapping it.

7. Stitch the tape to the two sides of the quilt, approximately ⅛" (3.2mm) inside the edge of the quilt.

TIP: These finishing techniques are best practices for me, but not every step may be necessary for you. Quilts that are not intended to hang do not need sleeves. Twill tape gives quilts extra structure, but your quilt might not need it. If you do not want to add it, don't. If you want to make a different kind of binding, go ahead. As my quilting friends say, done is better than perfect!

Make the Binding

To determine how much binding to make, measure the perimeter of the quilt, then add 10" (25.4cm). If we use our example of a 32" x 25" (81.3 x 63.5cm) quilt, the perimeter is 114" (2.9m): 32" + 32" + 25" + 25" + 10" = 124" (81.3cm + 81.3cm + 63.5cm + 63.5cm + 25.4cm = 3.2m). You would need to make a binding that is at least 124" (3.2m) long.

Cut as many 2¼" (5.7cm) width-of-fabric strips as you need to go around the quilt. I use a straight-grain binding, rather than a bias binding. Since stitched mosaic quilts are usually wall hangings and do not get handled and washed often, a straight-grain binding

1. Place one strip down horizontally in front of you so that the right-hand side of the strip is the working end. The printed side of the fabric should be facing up.

2. Place a second strip on top of the first at a 90-degree angle, with the right sides of the fabrics facing each other. This time, the top of the strip is the working end. Make sure that there is a little overlap on all the ends. Look at the four corners of the overlap to double-check that the strips are truly at right angles.

3. Draw a diagonal line from the top left corner to the bottom right corner.

Pinning on either side of your drawn line will help secure the two binding strips together while you sew.

5. Stitch the pieces together along the marked line.

6. Trim off the excess strips, ¼" (6.4mm) outside of the stitched line.

Your sewn and trimmed edge should be a sharp 45-degree angle.

Pressing the seam to one side will keep the joints of your binding strips even.

8. Add as many strips as needed.

9. Press the binding in half lengthwise, with the right side out.

Attach the Binding

Once the binding is prepared, you'll have to machine stitch it to the right side of the quilt.

1. Starting in the middle of one side, place one end of the binding on top of the front of the quilt with the raw edges of the binding lined up on top of the trimmed quilt edge.

2. Using a ¼" (6.4mm) seam allowance, stitch the binding in place approximately 10" (25.4cm) from the beginning end

of the binding. The unsewn "tail" will be used to join the ends of the binding later. In the Join the Ends step 1 photo on page 110, I started sewing with the blue fabric and moved clockwise around the quilt, ending with the orange

Corners

Corners can be difficult, but once you learn a few tricks, you can make perfect corners every time.

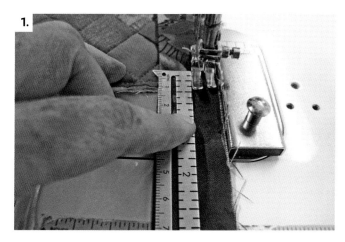

1. Stitch along the first edge of the quilt, stopping ¼" (6.4mm) from the corner of the quilt **with the needle down**. Sometimes it is hard to eyeball where that ¼" spot is. You can mark it with a pencil or hold a ruler next to the presser foot for guidance.

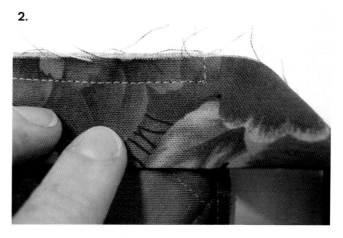

2. With the needle still in the quilt, lift the presser foot and rotate the quilt 90 degrees counterclockwise. Backstitch off the edge of the quilt. This extra backstitching helps create a perfect mitered corner. Break your thread and remove the quilt from under the presser foot.

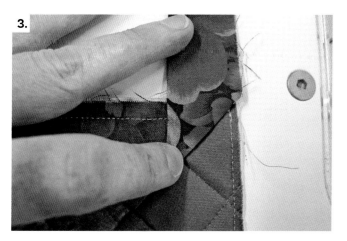

3. Fold the working tail of the binding up and back on itself. The fold should be at a 45-degree angle from the corner of the quilt, and the raw edge of the binding should line up with the next edge to be sewn.

4. Now fold the binding back down, covering the mitered corner. The top fold of the binding should lay along the top edge of the quilt, making a perfect right angle. Pin the folded corner in place.

5.

5. Starting at the top edge of the quilt, stitch the binding on with a ¼" (6.4mm) seam allowance. Stitch the length of

When the binding is folded around the quilt, it will create a perfect mitered corner.

Join the Ends

After you have turned the fourth corner on your quilt, stitch until about 10" (25.4cm) from where you started sewing on the binding, leaving an opening. Each end of the binding should have about 10" of "extra" tail.

1.

2.

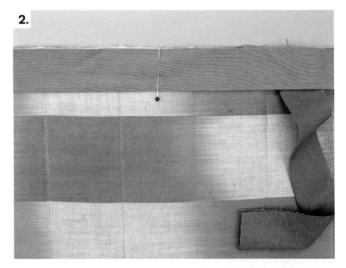

1. Place the quilt on a flat surface so that the edge you are working on is away from you. The bulk of the quilt will be in your lap.

2. Lay the left tail (in this case, the orange tail) down flat on the quilt's edge and smooth it out. Approximately halfway between the beginning and ending stitched points of the binding, pin through the top layer of the left tail perpendicular to the quilt edge.

3.

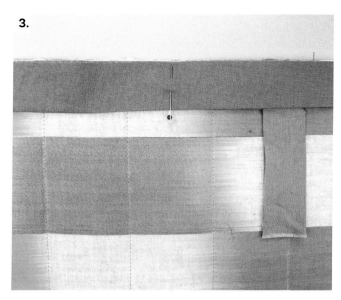

3. Place the right tail (the blue tail) on top of the left tail and smooth it out. Put a second pin through the top layer of the right tail so that the pins stack directly on top of each other.

4.

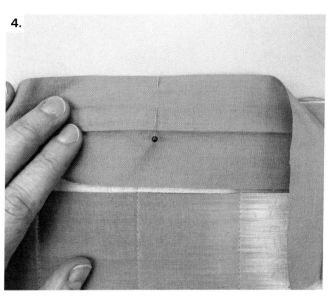

4. Open up the left tail and place it down so that it is horizontal, and the right side of the fabric is face up.

5.

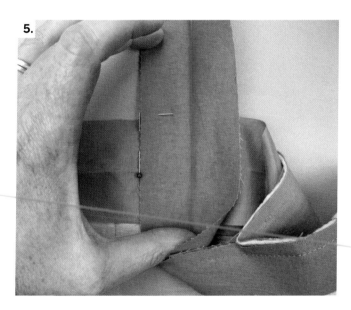

5. Open up the right-tail, rotate it 90 degrees clockwise, then flip it over so the right side of the fabric is facing down. The working end will point up. Line up the tails so that their pins come together at a 90-degree angle, with each fabric edge lying parallel against the pin in the other tail. (The pin in the right tail should be parallel to the quilt edge, while the pin in the left tail should be perpendicular to the quilt edge.) You will need to scrunch up the quilt a bit at this point to have enough slack for everything to line

6.

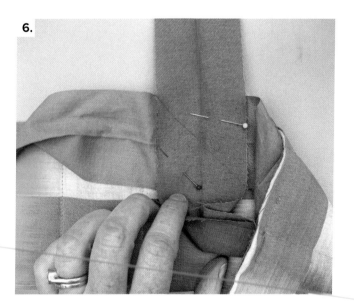

6. Draw a pencil line from the upper left corner to the bottom right corner. Pin on either side of the line to hold

TIP: On small quilts, I attach a hanging sleeve before stitching the binding to the back of the quilt.

7.

7. Remove pins and open the binding. Make sure the binding is the correct length (and that you did not accidentally twist it while pinning). Once you have confirmed that it is correct, trim the extra tails off ¼" (6.4mm) from the stitched line. Press the seam to one side.

8.

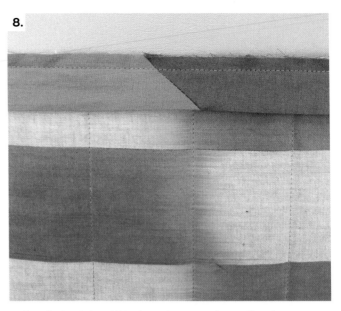

8. Stitch the joined binding down to the quilt edge, leaving a ¼" (6.4mm) seam allowance.

9.

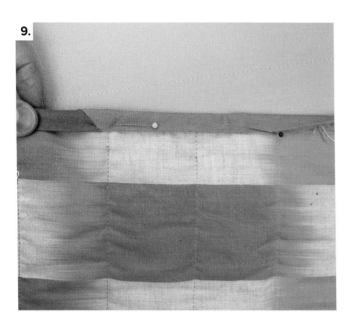

9. To cover all the raw edges, turn the folded edge of the binding to the back of the quilt. Pull the binding tight against the edge of the quilt to avoid creating a floppy edge. Hand stitch the binding to the back of the quilt using a hem stitch. The binding will also cover the twill tape.

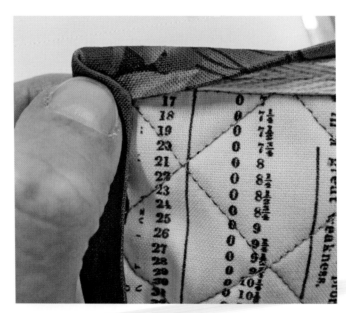

When turning the corners to the back of the quilt, manipulate them until you get a 45-degree miter edge. Pin your corners in place while you hand stitch them down.

Adding Hanging Sleeves

For small quilts, my sleeves finish at 2½" (6.4cm) tall. For larger quilts, or any that may hang in a quilt show and need to accommodate larger hanging rods, my sleeves finish at 4¼" (10.8cm) tall.

1. Measure the width of the quilt and subtract 3" (7.6cm). This number is the length of fabric you need for your sleeve piece. For a 2½" (6.4cm) sleeve, this length of fabric should be 5½" (14cm) wide. So, to add a 2½" sleeve to a 32" (81.3cm) wide quilt, the sleeve fabric would be cut to 29" x 5½" (73.7 x 14cm). For a 4¼" (10.8cm) sleeve, this fabric strip should be 9" (22.9cm) wide. So, to add a 4¼" sleeve to a 32" (81.3cm) wide quilt, the sleeve fabric would be cut to 29" x 9" (73.7 x 22.9cm).

2. Hem the 5½" (14cm) or 9" (22.9cm) ends of the sleeve by folding the edges under ¼" (6.4mm), then folding them again to hide the raw edges. Then stitch the hem down.

3. Fold the sleeve in half lengthwise, with the right sides out.

4. Center the sleeve on the top edge of the back of the quilt and pin it in place. Then stitch the sleeve in place ⅛" (3.2mm) inside the edge of the quilt.

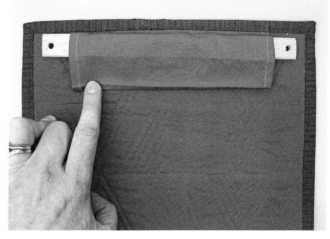

Your final sleeve should be secure, but loose enough that the hanging rod can easily be inserted without affecting the front of the quilt.

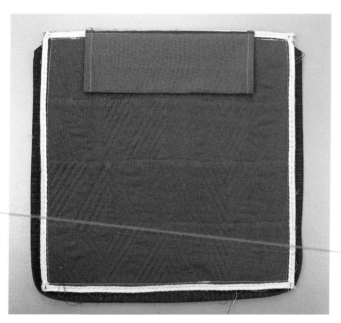

Adding hanging sleeves before stitching the binding to the back of the quilt will allow for a cleaner and more secure result.

5. Fold the binding around to the back of the quilt and hand stitch it in place. Stitch through the binding and sleeve layers, trying to catch the quilt backing and batting every few stitches to anchor all the layers.

6. To attach the bottom of the sleeve to the quilt, fold the bottom crease of the sleeve up towards the top of the sleeve by ¼" (6.4mm) and pin it in place. Hand stitch along the new fold line using a hem stitch. This extra fold adds a little ease to the sleeve to more easily insert a hanging rod.

TIP: Add a label to the back of your quilt. The label can include any information you want to keep with the quilt and can be as simple or as intricate as you want to make it. My labels include the name of the quilt, the year I made it, my name and town, and my contact info.

To make the label, I use a pen capable of writing on fabric, such as a Pigma Micron® pen or a Pentel Gel Roller for Fabric pen, to write on a piece of material. Before writing, iron a piece of freezer paper to the back of the label to stabilize the fabric and make the writing smoother. After writing, remove the freezer paper, turn the edges of the label under ¼" (6.4mm) on each side. Pin the label in place and hand stitch it to the back of the quilt.

Templates

I've included original photos and simplified illustrations for all the projects featured in the book, including the Blue Daisy and Rhubarb Leaf practice projects in Chapter 3. You can copy and enlarge either image, depending on what will work best for you. I've also provided enlargement guidance to match the project instructions, but if you'd like to attempt making larger or smaller quilts with these designs, print them at larger or smaller sizes.

Cheeky Cat photo template
Copy and enlarge by 248% to print at 18" x 18" (45.7 x 45.7cm)

Cheeky Cat illustration
Copy and enlarge by 248% to print at 18" x 18" (45.7 x 45.7cm)

Charming Chicken photo template
Copy and enlarge by 248% to print at 18" x 18" (45.7 x 45.7cm)

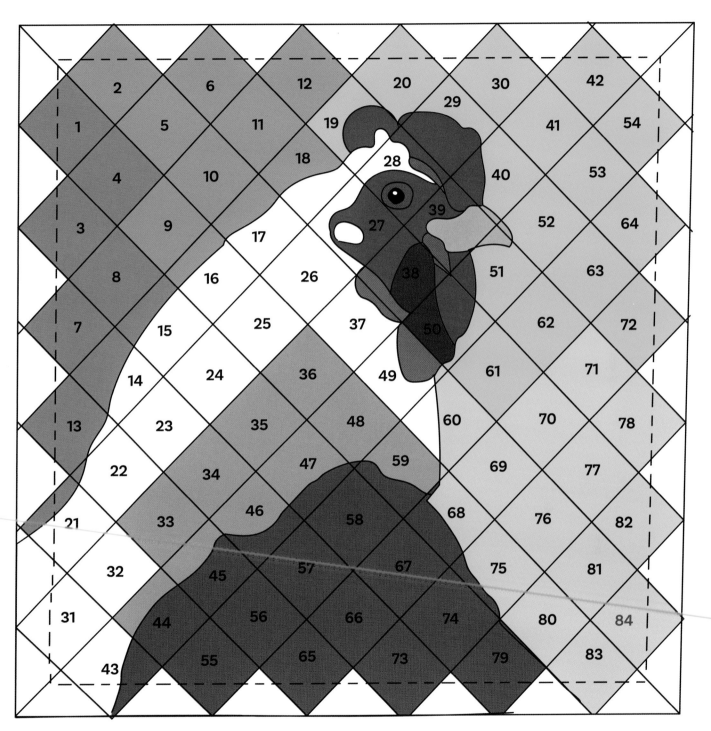

Charming Chicken illustration

Copy and enlarge by 248% to print at 18" x 18" (45.7 x 45.7cm)

Dashing Dog photo template
Copy and enlarge by 331% to print at 24" x 18" (61 x 45.7cm)

Dashing Dog illustration
Copy and enlarge by 331% to print at 24" x 18" (61 x 45.7cm)

Bearded Iris photo template
Copy and enlarge by 400% to print at 24" x 36" (61 x 91.4cm)

Bearded Iris illustration
Copy and enlarge by 400% to print at 24" x 36" (61 x 91.4cm)

Blue Daisy photo template
Copy and enlarge by 165% to print at 12" x 12" (30.5 x 30.5cm)

Blue Daisy illustration

Copy and enlarge by 165% to print at 12" x 12" (30.5 x 30.5cm)

Rhubarb Leaf photo template
Copy at 121% to print at 8½" x 11" (21.6 x 27.9cm)

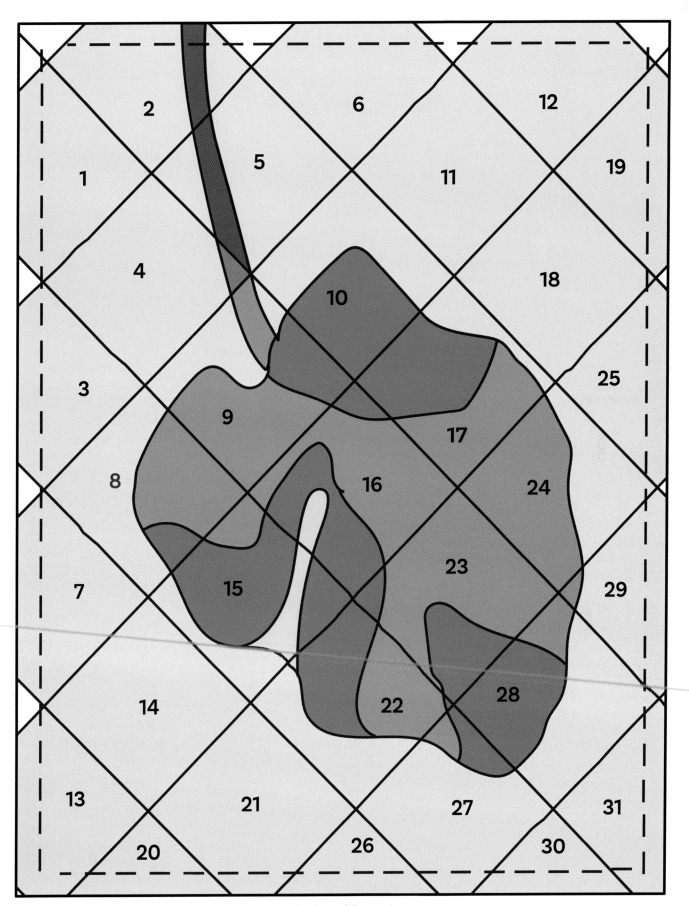

Rhubarb Leaf illustration
Copy at 121% to print at 8½" x 11" (21.6 x 27.9cm)

About the Author

Timna Tarr is an award-winning quilter best known for her use of color and her stitched mosaic technique. Timna comes from a long line of quilters but did not begin quilting until after receiving a BA in art history from the University of Massachusetts Amherst. After buying her first longarm quilting machine in 2001, she quilted for clients for 15 years. Timna is an in-demand teacher and speaker whose work has been showcased on *The Quilt Show* and *Quilting Arts TV* and featured in many publications. She is also a designer for Studio e Fabrics. Timna lives in western Massachusetts with her husband, teenage daughter, and a cheeky cat. To learn more about Timna and to see her work, visit *www.TimnaTarr.com*, or follow her on Instagram

Photo Credits

Index